# The Barefoot Fisherman

by
Paul Amdahl

# The Barefoot Fisherman
# by Paul Amdahl

## Copyright 2000

## This edition published in 2014 by

## London and Stout Publishing
### in cooperation with the author

Originally published by
Clearwater Publishing Company
original ISBN:0692202145

ISBN 0-927815-0-9

Cover Design by
A Figure of Speech

*This book is dedicated in loving memory to my Grandma,
Leatrice Schumacher*

Special thanks to:

My dad Kenn Amdahl for introducing me to the whole publishing process and all his help with this project; my mom Cheryl Amdahl for editing; my brother Scott for help with editing and answering my general questions about writing; my brother Joey for letting me use his picture; Gregg Schumacher for editing; Danny Schumacher for editing and the use of his picture; Alex Schumacher for her pictures,

Kent Madden from Gart Sports who taught me about fishing tackle;

Steve Smith for editing;

Adria Ellerbrock from A Figure of Speech, Inc. who designed the cover and the web site;

Jim Fay for writing the preface;

Jan Finger and *In Fisherman Magazine* for pictures on pages 14, 32, 33, 60, 65, 72, 79, 81, 84, 85, 87, 123, 124,127;

John Wilson from Alaska's Lake Marie Lodge for pictures on pages 12, 95, 99, 100, www.lakemarie.com;

Rainbow Lodge and everyone in their pictures including Leslie Holmes and Dustin Forington, for pictures on pages 36, 125;

Gerald Crawford at *Basstimes* for pictures on pages 50, 55, 14, 61, 76, 89;

NOAA for picrures on pages 41 , 71, 75, 77, 83, 86, 90, 114, 115, 117, 118, 9, 120, 121, 126, 129,131;

U.S. Fish and Wildlife Service for pictures on pages 34, 35, 48;

Karen Anfinson and Pure Fishing for pictures on pages 16, 17, 18, 23, 30;

Stan Orr for the picture on page 9 and all his support.

# Contents

# Preface

My good friend, Paul Amdahl, has visited our lake high in the Colorado Rockies several times. I always marvel at how he can catch fish even when others spend lots of time casting and reeling in empty hooks and lures. He knows how to think like a bug and think like a fish so that he knows best how to trick the wily trout.

He visited the lake the other day and asked a favor of me, "Jim, you know a lot about fishing because you have fished for over 50 years. You know a lot about kids because you have worked with kids and families for over 45 years. And you know a lot about writing books because you have written many of them. I'd like you to read my new book about fishing and let me know what you think of it. I wrote it especially for kids because so many of the fishing books are written for old guys."

I agreed, but had to say, "I can do it but not for the next few months. I'm just finishing a new book of my own and don't have time for this one just yet. Be patient and I will read it in a couple of months."

What do you know? It rained and hailed that evening so I couldn't go out on the lake so I decided to read a few pages of The Barefoot Fisherman. Uh-oh, now I was in trouble. I couldn't quit turning the pages. It was a great read. Better than that, I was learning all kinds of things I didn't know. All through the evening, I kept wishing that he had written the book 50 years ago so the kid in me could have learned from this master fisherman.

Early the next day my friend, Dr. Foster Cline, the great child psychiatrist, arrived at our lake. I was so excited. "Foster, don't go down to the lake yet. You have to read this new book and tell me what you think."

Soon Dr. Cline was just like a little kid, yelling, "Jim, this is great! I learn something on every page. You've got to encourage Paul to get this published right away!"

I'm happy to be one of the first to read The Barefoot Fisherman. I bet you'll love it as much as I do. I hope that when you are my age you can look back and remember The Barefoot Fisherman and how much joy it put into your life. I hope you discover that every time you cast your line the little kid in you who loves to fish never goes away.

-- Jim Fay
Co-author of *Parenting with Love and Logic,* and many others.

*Jim Fay with a nice trout*

# The Barefoot Fisherman

The young boy made his way through the weeds as the sun rose slowly over the horizon. Grasshoppers and beetles shook off the morning dew and started about their daily routines. Soon the weeds gave way to cattails yet the marshy land did not slow the boy's approach. One of his feet went splashing down into a hidden water hole. He pulled it out with a sucking sound as the pond mud tried to hold onto his shoe. The sound of his sneaker in the mud startled a frog, which jumped into the pond.

He had fished this pond a couple of times and never had much luck. As he stood at the water's edge, his shadow fell upon a turtle swimming in the water. The turtle disappeared in the blink of an eye. The boy looked through a cluttered tackle box, and selected a large metal spoon. When he was done tying it on there was a knot that looked like spaghetti around a fork.

He cast the lure as far as he could, confident that the biggest fish were in the middle of the lake.

He fished for a while, watching water-bugs swim among the duckweed. Through the water he saw a craw-dad emerge from under a rock kicking up little puffs of mud-smoke with its tail. Somewhere in the cattails he heard the big splash of a bass eating something.

He knew that under the water's ripples lurked huge catfish. The splash of the bass told him that the fish were hungry, yet he still had no bites.

After a hundred or so casts and twice as many mosquito bites the boy decided to call it a morning. He gathered up his fishing pole and reassembled his tackle box. It had been a pleasant trip but as he walked along the dirt road back to civilization, he wore a frown. If he could just figure out how to catch those fish...

*A nice salmon*

# Chapter One: Fishing is Fun

Have you ever filled a blender with dead grass-hoppers in order to make the flavor-juice for your carp bait? I have.

On rainy mornings I walk the streets with a coffee can picking up earthworms for my afternoon fishing trips. When worms are scarce, squid tentacles work to catch largemouth bass. And nearly any bait will catch the strange fish that live and feed on the bottom of the ocean.

Fishing is a mixture of all the things that are fun about being a kid. There are bugs, and animals and hope and excitement, there are sometimes stars and friends and every fishing trip somehow ends up as a story that you will tell over and over again.

If you like adventure you'll like to fish. Whether you are going after the ferocious largemouth bass or the bottom-dwelling whiskered catfish, you will come home with dirt-covered hands and a smile on your face.

Anyone can fish but some people catch more fish than others. This is because they understand fish better. They have an advantage. They can look at a lake or river and tell where the fish are, what kind of fish there are, and what they are eating. They know the secrets of fishing. Luckily, anybody can learn these secrets. Some people have parents or grandparents who can pass these secrets on to them. Some people don't know anybody who can tell them where to find the biggest trout in a river or how cloud-cover affects fishing action. These people must learn on their own. It's a shame because they will not catch nearly as many fish. It will take them years to learn through trial and error and they might even get discouraged and quit fishing for lack of success. Well, I love fishing and I couldn't stand to see that happen to anybody. I am one of the lucky ones who had a dad and two grandpas who taught me the secrets of fishing. This book contains the secrets that will allow you to catch as many fish as anyone, probably a lot more.

# Chapter Two
# Reels, Rods, and Line

The guys who really know what they're doing when it comes to fishing (and I'm talking about the guys that are winning the Bass Masters tournaments and the guys that are hauling in world record fish) all have something in common: they all understand their equipment. They know why they use a bait caster for one set of circumstances and an open-faced spinning outfit for others. And it shows. The rod, reel, and the line make up the basics of your gear. These are more important than what lure you use. You can always switch lures.

### *Reels*
Reels hold the line and they reel in the line. A good reel doesn't get tangled and doesn't inhibit your casting distance. If you want to cast far enough to reach the big ones jumping in the middle, choose your reel carefully. The three basic kinds are closed-faced spinning, open-faced spinning, and bait casting.

*A closed faced reel*

### Closed Faced Spinning Reels

Most people learn to fish with a closed-faced spinning reel. Beginners choose them for their simplicity. To cast, press your thumb on the button during the back swing. As you swing the rod forward, let go of the button.

Closed faced spin cast reels get tangled sometimes and often won't reel in if there isn't tension on the line. To fix this periodic problem, while you reel in your line, pull the line to create tension going into the reel.

If your line gets tangled inside the reel casing, don't be afraid to open it up and fix the problem. The inner workings are simple to understand and easy to put back together. A good closed-faced, spin-cast reel to start with, is the Zebco 202.

## Open Faced Spinning Reels

Open-faced, spinning reels cast light weights a great distance. They are easy to use, but some people think they look complicated. When casting, grab the string with your pointer finger keeping a tight line between the reel and your finger. Use your other hand to open the bail, then cast (pull back and swing forward and when you're swinging forward, let go of the line with your pointer finger). Open-faced spinning reels don't get tangled very often because they have oscillating spools (the spool moves back and forth as you reel) that wrap line on evenly.

*Open faced spinning reel*

Bait-casting reels are good for accuracy casting. Bass fishermen choose bait-casters because they allow them to pinpoint cast a lure between weeds, under docks, or next to trees.

Bait-casting reels operate differently than either the open-faced spinning reel or the closed faced spinning reel (both types are also called spin-casters). Spin-casters have a stationary spool of line. When a cast is made, the line peels off the spool. Bait-casters have a spool that turns.

The problem with bait-casters is that it takes a little practice to learn how to cast one. This is because you have to control the speed the spool is turning with your thumb, and you have to stop it from spinning when your cast is complete. If you don't do this, (and it is not easy) your line will become tangled. If you want to learn how to cast with a bait casting reel, take it out to a park, and practice a few times before you go fishing. You don't want to waste a day's fishing learning how to cast and untangling line.

## Reel Basics

The three basic reel designs all share certain features that can make one reel more appealing than another. Reels have varying gear ratios. Gear ratios determine how much line is retrieved with each turn of the reel handle. The larger the ratio, (5:1 compared to 3:1) the faster you can reel in line.

All reels also come equipped with a drag setting. (Drag is resistance to the line coming out of the reel.) There is usually a knob that you can turn to tighten or loosen the drag. The drag can be set so that when a fish pulls hard, the reel lets line out. This way the line doesn't break. If no line was allowed to come out of the reel, a fish could just pull until he pulled hard enough to break the line. With the drag set properly, when a fish pulls softly nothing changes, the line doesn't go out. But if the fish pulls hard enough to break the line, the reel lets line out so the fish can't break it.

You can set your drag to let line out at whatever tension you want. Experiment with different tensions until you find a setting you like. Learning how to use your drag will allow you to catch much heavier fish. If you get a 45-pound catfish to bite when using 6-pound line, you have a chance of catching him if your drag is set right. If your drag is not set right, then he will probably break your line when he feels the hook.

*Rods*

A fishing rod (or fishing pole) is what fights the fish. The fish is pulling against the rod. This is what tires the fish out. The stiffness of the rod affects how much resistance the fish has to pull against. You don't want the rod to be so soft that it gets bent all the way over because you won't be able to move the fish. If the rod is too stiff you won't be able to detect strikes as well, The stiffness of the rod also determines to an extent how far you can cast. Stiff rods generally cast farther.

When you pick out a fishing rod, you should get one that is comfortable for you to hold. Find one that is not too stiff and not too soft. You'll undoubtedly go through several rods in your life so don't worry too much about it. Some species of fish require certain rods. For example, you wouldn't fish for Halibut with a Snoopy rod, and likewise you wouldn't fish for sunfish with a surf rod. Choose a versatile rod that allows you to fish for the kinds of fish in your neighborhood. The fishing rod is a tool; it shouldn't get in the way of your fishing.

Fishing line can make the difference between a long cast and a short one, between landing a lunker (a huge fish) and telling stories about the one that got away.

Different types of line include monofilament, braided, and lead-core. Monofilament is the clear line that you probably are most familiar with. Braided lines look more like string and tend to be very strong. Lead core lines will sink quickly to the depths of a lake when trolling from a boat. The versatility of monofilament makes it the choice of most people. Experiment with different brands to choose your favorite.

Step one in choosing a line is matching the fishing line to the reel and pole. Fishing line comes in different sizes. These sizes are the weight that will break the line. For example, 4-pound line will break if you hang a 4-pound weight from it. This doesn't mean that it would take a four-pound fish to break the line. A one pound fish can pull harder than 4-pounds and can break your line.

Danny Schumacher with his trout

However by setting the drag, you can catch fish much larger than the line weight.

The recommended line weight will be written on the reel. Don't try to put 30-pound line on a reel that supposed to hold 6-pound. It wont cast right and will get tangled. As a rule of thumb, always use the lightest line possible. The lighter the line the farther it will cast.

*Alex Schumacher with a trout*

When you fill the reel with line, look at the side of the spool to see what size line is recommended for that size reel. Fill the spool until the line is approximately 1/8 of an inch from the edge. At this point the reel will cast the farthest without getting tangled.

Change your line every year. Monofilament line gets weakened from use and even loses some of its strength just sitting around.

Before each fishing trip it's a good idea to run the last couple of feet of line through your fingers. If you feel tiny snags and nicks in the line, cut off the damaged end. The worst time to discover that the end of your line needed trimming is when a big fish breaks it.

*Monofiliment line should be replaced every year or so*

# Chapter Three
## Tackle

I've always been fascinated with tackle boxes and what's inside them. Whenever I go fishing with someone new I always try to get a peek into his or her tackle box. I think it's because a tackle box is kind of like a treasure chest. Popping the lid open reveals all sorts of shiny, colorful trinkets. So of course I love to get stuff to put into my tackle box.

*Looking for the perfect lure....*

*Found it!*

The tackle box can be your pockets or it could be a giant plastic box that holds much more tackle than you need. Think about where you might go fishing and visualize yourself carrying that tackle box. If you hike somewhere to fish, you don't want your tackle box to be too big or heavy. Of course, if every time you open it everything spills out, that's no good either. I use a soft-shelled tackle box that has a strap that goes over my shoulder. This allows me to hike comfortably while keeping one hand free. If you're carrying your fishing pole in one hand and a plastic tackle box in the other, you can't use your hands to climb. With my tackle box over my shoulder, I can use my free hand to grab branches, or to steady myself against rocks as I climb to the perfect spot. You could use almost anything (that would hold your stuff) for a tackle box: a grocery bag, a shoebox, or whatever. As long as it is comfortable for you, then why not?

I sometimes daydream about how I would catch fish if I was stranded on a desert island. There wouldn't be many supplies on the island maybe some plants and seashells and rocks and stuff. When you think about it all you would really need to make would be fishing line, hooks, weights, and maybe a bobber. The basic tackle in a tackle box includes hooks, weights, and bobbers. With these three necessities you are ready to catch fish.

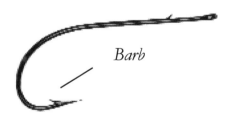

*Barb*

*Hooks*

Hooks come in many different shapes and sizes. Some shapes are better for certain situations but the basic hook can be used in most cases. Hooks are simple. The eye of the hook is where you tie the line on. The barb of the hook keeps the hook from sliding out of the fish's mouth after you hook him. The barb also makes it harder to unhook a fish. Many fishermen, including me, pinch the barb flat with a pair of needle-nosed pliers so that it will be easier to let fish go. A flattened barb allows the hook to penetrate easier resulting in more hooked fish. The point of the hook needs to be sharp. Some fisherman sharpen their hooks periodically to insure that they are sharp. The size of hook is determined by the size of the fish you are fishing for. Choose a hook that is not too large for the mouth of the fish you seek. Small hooks work well to catch big fish, don't worry that your hook will be too small. It is rare that a fish will straighten your hook. It's much more likely that your knot will give out or your line will break before a lunker straightens your hook.

Some hooks have strange twists and bends in them. I recommend that you stay away from these cheapies. I don't know if they make it harder to hook a fish or not, but neither do you. It's no fun to wonder, while you're fishing, if it's your fault that you missed a fish, or the hooks. So get good hooks.

Fishing weights (also called sinkers) allow you to cast your line and make it sink once in the water. Sometimes it takes more weight to sink your bait to the bottom. This is especially important when you fish in a river. River current moves at different speeds in different places. If you want your bait to stay near the bottom you'll need the right amount of weight to keep it down. Split-shot weights pinch shut around your line, and can be pinched open for removal. This makes it easy to add or take off weights. Years ago some people (including me) used to use their teeth to open and close split-shot. Now we know this isn't a good idea because split shot are made out of lead, and lead is poisonous. It won't kill you right away, but the microscopic particles that break off into your mouth build up in your system and eventually cause problems for some people. Use needle-nosed pliers instead, to open and close split shot.

Sinkers come in many different shapes. Some are round (like split-shots) some are torpedo shaped with a hole going through them. These are good for fishing with rubber worms, because they slide up and down on your line. This makes the rubber worm move though the water in different ways depending on your retrieve (the way you reel in line.)

Pyramid-shaped weights are used for surf fishing the ocean. They burrow into the ocean sand to hold your bait on the bottom in spite of the strong ocean current. There are also egg-shaped weights and teardrop-shaped weights. I like to have some of each kind including some tiny split shots. They just seem to come in handy.

*The size and shape of the sinker determines how it works*

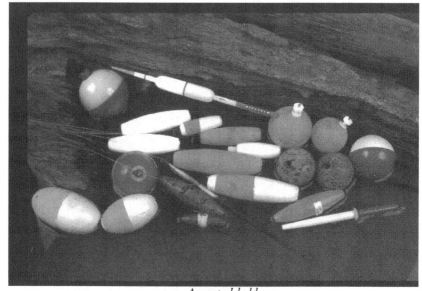

*Assorted bobbers*

### *Bobbers*

Bobbers or floats, suspend your bait in the water. A bobber can be a piece of cork or Styrofoam or anything that floats. Stores sell several different styles of plastic ones. Use a bobber when you want to keep your bait from sinking all the way to the bottom. If you don't have a bobber you can always make one out of cattails or a stick.

I sometimes use round, colored bobbers, and other times the clear bubble ones that fill up partially with water. These cast much farther without adding weights. I use this when fishing a dry fly and bubble combination.

*Fishing Tools*

Tools that make fishing easier include needle-nosed pliers which are useful for removing the hook from a fish's mouth and for opening and closing split-shots.

A pocketknife comes in handy all the time. If you need to gut a fish you'll need a knife.

Fingernail clippers are great for trimming your line. I keep some on a chain I wear around my neck. That way, they are always where I can use them.

I keep a lighter or matches for making a campfire. If you are going to kill some of the fish you catch, you should bring a club. A miniature baseball bat would work well. Though not a necessity, it is nice to have a towel to dry your hands with after you've handled a wet fish, especially if it is cold outside. I keep a washcloth in my tackle box.

*Trout are found in cold water*

# Chapter Four:
# Warm and Cold Water

You wouldn't expect to see a penguin walking down a street on a day so hot that the tar has turned to goo. Nor would you see a cactus growing on the frozen tundra of the Siberian wasteland. Similarly you will not find a largemouth bass in the cold waters of a mountain stream or a trout in the warm water of a Florida farmer's pond. Certain fish live in certain water temperatures. Some species of fish live in warm water, and others in cold water, some live in both. If the lake or river stays relatively warm year round it will contain warm water fish. If the lake is deep enough to have cold water at the bottom (or if it stays cold all year) you will find cold water fish in it. Bass, crappie, sunfish, carp, and catfish live in warm water. Trout, pike, walleye, muskie, and suckers live in cold.

After a little practice you will begin to be able to tell the difference between a warm water lake or river and a cold one. Knowing what types of fish inhabit a body of water determines what type of tackle you will use to fish it.

Some signs that indicate you're at a warm-water lake or river include cattails, reeds, and other types of plants growing along the shore. You will see various

*Largemouth bass are found in warm water*

insects, in and out of the water. There are also frogs, turtles, birds, and snakes. The water feels slightly cool or even warm to the touch. Cold water lakes usually have pine trees around them and not as many water-bugs as warm water lakes. Also, if you put your hand in the water, it is really cold. The surface of a cold water lake generally freezes or partially freezes in the winter.

Once you figure out what kind of water you're dealing with, you have a good idea of what species of fish might live there. This will help you decide what tackle you use. If you're at a warm water pond you might use

*A typical warm water pond*

*A typical cold water pond*

a lure that looks like a frog. Warm water fish are used to eating frogs since frogs live in warm water lakes.

At a cold water lake you might try a fly pattern that represents a type of fly that lives in that area.

Understanding the environment the fish live in allows you to present bait that is consistent with the fish's normal everyday diet.

*Look at the size of this pike!*

# Chapter Five:
# Approach to the Water

Some people seem to catch more fish than everyone else. Some of it's luck, some of it's where they're fishing but most of it is how they walked up to the water.

Walking carelessly to the water is like sending a fire-truck ahead of you with its lights and sirens warning the fish to go hide. Fish don't seem to get scared by noises but they get startled easily by vibrations that travel from the ground into the water. If you stomp your foot or step on a loose rock that shifts, you might even see the fish swim for cover. Now they are spooked and less likely to eat anything, especially something that is at all different from their natural diet. When you approach your fishing spot, whether it is a stream or lake, walk slowly and softly. Don't step on loose rocks or logs.

As you walk carefully to the water you might notice other things that will help you catch fish. If there are frogs along the shore, you might guess that the fish eat frogs from time to time. The same goes for grasshoppers and other insects and animals. Sometimes as you walk near the water you might see puffs of mud smoke in the water. These are caused by fish that were startled by your approach and quickly swam away. Startled fish indicate you didn't walk gently enough. It also tells you that there are fish in the water and just knowing that makes me feel better.

Although fish live in the water, they notice what is happening on the shore. They can see above the water. That's how they can eat flies out of the air and that's how they can see you standing there. It seems that they focus on movement. When I am standing still the fish in front of me go about their business as usual but when I swing my arms to cast often they dart away. Avoid unnecessary sudden movements when near the shore.

Try to keep from casting your shadow or the shadow of your pole on the water, as this will also scare the fish. Any shadow that appears suddenly could be some animal hungry for fish. This will send the fish darting for the shelter of deep water. By not casting a shadow you're greatly improving your chances of catching fish. It's amazing how many fishermen don't know this or don't care, but they never seem to catch many fish.

The whole living world of a lake is connected; disturbing any part of it affects it all. For example, if you walk noisily up to the edge of a pond and scare a frog on the shore into the water, the fish know to be careful because something's wrong. If birds perched on cattails take flight suddenly when you approach, the fish will know you are there. In a way, all these different living things are looking out for each other.

Your first few casts are your best chance to catch a fish, since if you walked quietly they don't know you're there. It is also your best chance of catching an old fish. The older a fish is the smarter and the bigger he is. Unfortunately these are the hardest to catch because they get spooked the easiest. Take your time, it's worth it.

*My brother Joey with a bass*

# Chapter Six:
# Bait Fishing

Nestled on the bottom of a lake next to a rock a giant rainbow trout catches the movement of a wriggling worm. Its swaying motion beckons the huge fish closer; its worm smell causes the fish's stomach to growl. Thinking it has found an easy meal, the trout strikes.

### *Grasshoppers*

If you fish for trout, bass, or sunfish, sometimes the perfect bait is a grasshopper. Grasshoppers are a common food for fish, come in various sizes, and you can catch them near shore. Remember though, if you run around trying to catch grasshoppers, you're probably scaring the fish. Move far away from the water while catching them so you don't spook any lunkers.

A grasshopper makes brown stuff come out of its mouths when you catch it. It looks kind of scary, but it doesn't do anything to you. When you catch grasshoppers, try to not hurt them. A healthy grasshopper will kick across the water to get to the shore. That is what they would do if they accidentally fell in the water. The secret to fishing, is to make the bait look as natural as possible.

How do you hook the grasshopper so that he'll still be OK to swim around? Obviously you don't hook him through the head. If you're careful, you can put the hook through the thing that covers his neck (carapace). This doesn't seem to hurt the grasshopper much at all.

## Crawdads

Crawdads drive trout, bass, and many other kinds of fish, crazy. Crawdads, or crayfish, are crustaceans that can be found in both streams and lakes. They look like little lobsters three or four inches long. Crayfish are sensitive to light so they do most of their moving around and feeding at night. You find them under rocks or hiding in weeds. Crawdads shed their shells periodically. After a shedding the crawdad is called a peeler. It is during this stage that they make the best bait. (See "catching crawdads")

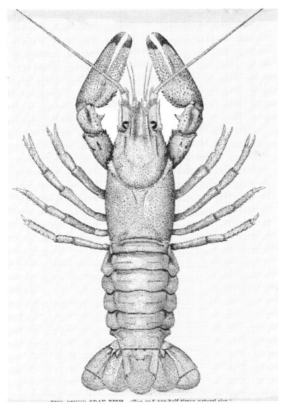

*Crawdads make great bait*

To hook a crawdad, place the hook through the tail. If you want the bait to be able to scoot backwards easily hook him through the back plate. Fish the crawdad along the bottom. Try to make it look as natural as possible. If you let the bait sit still for too long the little guy might crawl under a rock to hide from all those big fish. So be sure to reel in a little line every once in a while to bring the crawdad out in the open.

*Earthworms*

Earthworms and fishing go together like Saturday mornings and cartoons. Most species of fish can't resist the wiggle of the worm.

Earthworms can be found just about everywhere. After a rain they slither on the sidewalks. When it is dry, they hide underneath rocks and leaves.

Worms come in different varieties. Garden worms; red worms, jumping worms, and nightcrawlers might live in your yard. Nightcrawlers are much bigger than other kinds of worms. They get their name because they come out of their holes at night to eat. Nightcrawlers come out at night because it is cooler and the birds can't see them. Fishermen go on nightcrawler hunts after dark. The best places to look for nightcrawlers is on grass that has been recently watered. Golf courses are perfect. You need to sneak up on these giant worms because they can feel the vibrations of your footsteps and are quick to dart back down their holes.

Most people like to hook the worm twice while leaving a good part of the tail free to wiggle. When fishing for catfish or steelhead I like to use several worms on one hook. When fishing for walleye most fishermen hook the worm through the head, leaving the entire worm free to wiggle. Experiment to see what works best for you.

If you don't want to catch the worms yourself, you can buy them in a tackle store. When you buy a plastic container full of worms, instead of digging through it with your hand to retrieve some bait, set the container upside down with the lid on when you're not using it. The worms naturally go to the bottom, which is really the top, and when you're ready for one, just turn it over and open it up, and there they are, right on the top. *See "raising worms"

*Other baits*

While earthworms, grasshoppers, and crawdads rank among the best baits for many species of fish, there are lots of wonderful baits. Each person favors one type of bait over another with their own reasons for their preferences. Other common baits include corn, salmon eggs, doughbait, leeches, marshmallows, liver, etc.

*Corn*

Who would have ever thought that fish would eat corn? Let's face it you don't see too many trout in a Kansas corn field. But they love the stuff.

Corn is cheap; you can buy it at the grocery store, and whatever you don't use while fishing you can eat. Trout like corn, especially "stocked trout" which are accustomed to eating fish pellets in the fish hatchery.

Carp also like corn. Sometimes a little kernel of canned corn is the only thing a huge carp will bite, if the sunfish don't eat it first.

## Salmon eggs

What is red, comes packaged in a handy little jar, and catches fish like crazy? You guessed it... salmon eggs. Every time I open a jar of salmon eggs I smell it. The smell of salmon eggs takes me to a very happy place. I associate the scent with fishing and with good times.

Salmon eggs are an adult salmon's roe (roe means fish eggs) that has been processed to give them their bright red color. Salmon eggs are a standard bait for trout. They also work on sunfish, steelhead, salmon, and suckers. Each brand is a little different so experiment until you find something the fish will bite.

## Dough-bait

The angler (angler is a fancy word for fisherman) usually makes his own dough-bait. Dough-bait is a mixture of smelly substances worked into a hunk of dough. Dough-bait or dough-balls work best on catfish and carp although you surely could create versions for trout or other species of fish. (See catfish chapter for details.)

## Marshmallows

Marshmallows flavored with garlic or cheese are sold in most fishing stores. These will work on trout. Stores also sell different baits that rely on their smells to attract fish. Some of these work and some don't. Powerbait is one of most popular of these types of bait.

### Catching Crawdads

Even if you don't fish with them, crawdads are fun to catch. Their little pincers can pinch you if you're not careful, but that just adds to the excitement of catching them. Some people even fish for crawdads. Sometimes when you're fishing for fish, a big old crawdad clamps onto your line.

If you want to try and catch a crawdad with your line, tie a hook with worm, salmon egg, or some other bait on. Dangle it in the water by a rock where you think a crawdad lurks. Wait for him to come out and start gnawing your bait. Slowly pull in your line. He will think his food's escaping and he will clamp the line with one of his pincers. Then you can lift him up. They usually don't let go. Crawdads can live out of the water for a couple of minutes, but it is best to have a bucket full of water to put them in. They make great pets. You could set up an aquarium and put a couple crawdads in it. They're interesting to watch and help keep the bottom of the tank clean. Feed them little pieces of meat or earthworms.

Catching them by hand can be tricky. You'll probably need to wade, so make sure that there is no broken glass where you're wading. Rocks make great hiding places for crawdads. As you lift up the rock, the crawdad can get away. Lift up the rock slowly so you don't disturb too much mud and you'll be able to see where the little critter is headed. Pick up a crawdad from behind so he can't pinch you. Crawdads swim backwards, be ready for them to dart away once they see you coming.

If you're serious about catching them you could build a crawdad trap. The principle is the same as crabbing in the ocean. The trap is made of a fine wire mesh. This allows the smell of the bait to lure the crayfish in. Make a square box of wire mesh. On one side have a funnel opening so that the crawdads can get in but they will not be able to get out. You can use bits of meat for bait. Place the trap in a pond or stream facing the rocks or undercut bank where you think there are crawdads. Some people wrap the meat in cheesecloth to prevent the first crayfish from eating the bait before more are lured into the trap.

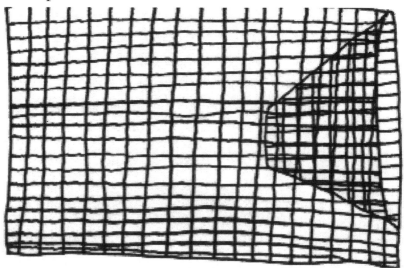

*A crawdad trap*

## Raising Worms

If you don't want to buy worms or dig them every time you go fishing, you could try raising them yourself. Raising worms sounds easy and fun, but there is more to it than you would think.

First you will need a container that is worm-proof, which means one that worms can't get out of. If you're going to try to raise worms, use a big container, not a coffee can or mayonnaise jar. You could build one out of wood, unless you just happen to have some container lying around that will work. If you use a big bucket, make sure that you clean and rinse it well. Any kind of animal that you try to raise, whether it's tropical fish or worms, is very sensitive to soap, chemicals, salt, or most anything. If you don't want them to die right away, make sure that the container is well rinsed off.

Once you have your container, probably the most important thing is where you put it. Worms need to be moist and cool, so you don't want to put it in direct sunlight. They would get too hot and they would bake. I learned that the hard way. Nothing smells worse then a vat of rotting baked worm goo. Find a place in the shade.

In a worm's natural state, the ground absorbs rainwater. When the ground becomes saturated the worms come out of their holes to the surface to breathe. That is why you can hunt them after a rain, and why they are on the sidewalks. But in a box, there is nowhere for the water to go. So it can fill up and drown the poor worms. You need to be able to regulate the amount of water

*Huge striped bass*

that is in the soil of your worm farm. To keep the right amount of moisture in the soil, it is a good idea to have some small pebbles at the bottom of the container. This allows the water to drain down. You should also have leaves on the top. They help to keep the dirt from drying out completely.

I think the best way to get dirt for your box is to look around your yard, find out where there are lots of worms, and then use that dirt. It's not a good idea to use store bought potting soil, because the fertilizers in it might burn the worms skin. I break up all big clumps of dirt so that the worms can dig in it easily. Worms don't like sand because it scratches their skin.

You will have to judge how many worms to start with. The size of your container should help you to decide. You don't want them to be too crowded. Once you have set up your worm farm, there is not much to do. Keep the dirt soft and moist but not too moist. If you designed it well, with moss or leaves on the top to keep the moisture in, you probably won't have to add water very often.

Be sure to feed your worms from time to time. They eat decomposing organic matter. Once a week, go out and sprinkle some coffee grounds on top or maybe put some oatmeal or an apple core in there.

Raising worms is really fun but I was never good at it. I always thought that if I could get it going, I could sell them to my friends who fished and start my own business. But I always ended up over watering my worms and drowning them or forgetting about them until they dried up. I hope you have more luck then I did. Remember that worms are living things. Do your best to take care of them.

# Chapter Seven:
# Lures

I remember walking up to the shore of a cold water trout lake. Along the bank fishermen were lined up, some sitting with their fishing poles resting on forked sticks, others standing up holding their poles. After a few minutes of talking to one of the fisherman it was apparent that the fishing was slow and no one had caught a fish in a long time. These bait fishermen sat there with their worms or salmon eggs resting on the bottom waiting for a bite. It was obvious to me that the popular method of fishing this lake at this time wasn't working. I guess it wasn't apparent to all these people that they should try a different approach.

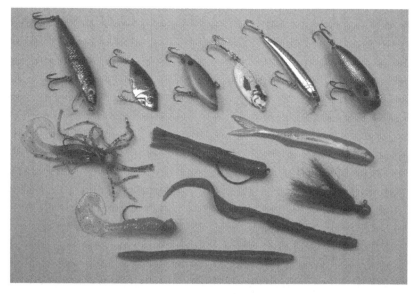

*Various lures*

People are creatures of habit and if they had luck with one method of fishing at one time they tend to always go back to it without trying new techniques. I am not guilty of this. Reaching into my tackle box I selected a Panther Martin spinner, the black one with yellow spots. After a couple of casts I caught a fish and then another and then another. I could see some of the other fisherman take notice and try to catch a glimpse of what I was using for bait.

It probably wasn't the particular lure I was using, I'm sure any number of lures would have taken trout that day. It was simply that the trout were not cruising the bottom smelling for bait. They were suspending in the water above the bottom and feeding on baitfish and aquatic insects. The moral to this story is simple ...if nobody is catching fish with one method of fishing, try something else. Lures offer a wide selection of things to try.

Lures imitate various natural foods of fish. Yet in many cases lures are much more effective that the real thing. The most obvious example that comes to mind is the artificial fly. It would be awfully tough to put a live mosquito onto a hook, but an artificial fly works great.

Lures don't fall off of the hook like bait. You can also bring a wide assortment of different lures where it is not always practical to bring lots of different types of bait. By retrieving at various speeds you can fish different depths of water easily with lures. You can also catch lots of fish with the same lure. You can reel in a lure much faster than you can with bait, maybe to trigger a bass to strike.

The lure gets all of its action from you. Try to imitate a natural fish-food. If you are using flies try to make the fly act just like a living fly would. If you are using a lure that looks like a little fish, then try to make the lure swim just like a little fish.

## Rubber Worms

It is hard to find a fish that doesn't start drooling fish drool all over himself at the sight of a worm. As well as natural earthworms work, artificial or rubber worms can be even more effective on certain kinds of fish.

There are as many varieties and colors of rubber worms as there are kinds of cookies. Just like sometimes you might want an Oreo and sometimes a chocolate chip,

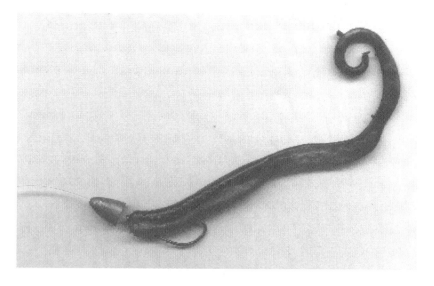

*A weedless rubber worm rigging with a sliding sinker*

sometimes a bass will bite a blue worm and other times a neon pink one. Aside from all the different colors, rubber worms come in different shapes and sizes, and in some cases, even smells.

Bass love rubber worms. In the hot months of summer, when the fish have gone down to the cool waters of the depths of a lake, a rubber worm jigged off the bottom is hard to beat. Cast the worm and allow it to sink. Once it is on the bottom raise your rod tip to cause the worm to lift a foot or two above the bottom. Then lower your rod tip and reel in the slack. Repeat this process until you've retrieved your lure and then try it again. Bass will often strike the worm while it is fluttering back down to the bottom. So if anything strange happens to your line, like it doesn't go slack or it moves, set the hook.

Rubber worms are usually fished with a sliding sinker rig. The rig can allow the weight to slide all the way down to the worm or it may have a swivel 18 inches above the worm to stop the sinker. The worm may be made to be "weedless" by twisting the hook and sticking the tip back into the worm. When a fish bites, the hook set will drive the point through the worm and hook the fish.

As I said, rubber worms come in many different colors. You might think that the worm should be the color of a earthworm to look natural but this is not the case. Rubber worms sometimes look like worms as you jig them off the bottom. Sometimes they remind a fish of a baitfish like a minnow or a perch or sunfish, and other times they don't look like any food at all.

For example, you can buy blue rubber worms with sparkles. Have you ever seen a blue sparkled worm in real life? Neither has the fish. The color allows the fish to see the worm easier under certain conditions. In muddy water, fish might not see an earthworm, but a bright orange rubber worm might catch their eye, and trigger a strike.

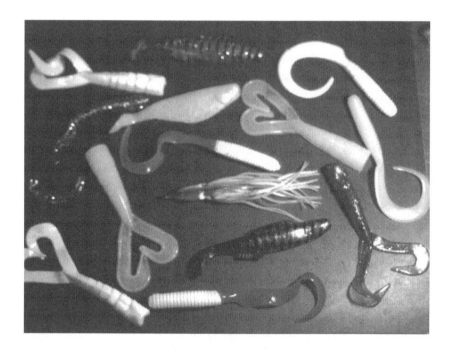

*Rubber worms come in all sorts of size and colorss*

# *Jigs*

It seems natural that fishing with a rubber worm and sliding sinker rig would lead some clever inventor to come up with the idea of attaching the weight to the hook, and sure enough someone did. Now we can add to our arsenal of lures the almighty jig. A jig is basically a hook with a lead weight for a head. The body can be feathers or rubber skirts or a rubber grub. Similar to rubber worms, jigs are fished off of the bottom in a series of short twitches of the rod tip.

People often tip their jigs with worms or minnows or leeches or pork rinds to give them added appeal. Although this is not necessary it seems to increase the interest of walleye in particular.

Jigs come in all sorts of colors and sizes and are effective on most saltwater and freshwater fish.

*A jig with a weed protector*

*A bass spinner*

## Spinners

When I walk up to a lake that I know little about, the first lure I try is usually a spinner. Spinners work well in various conditions, they work on many species of fish, and they can be fished in different ways depending on circumstances. Spinners are an all around lure.

A spinner consists of either a treble hook or sometimes a single hook, a body that is often made of metal beads or a single piece of lead and the blade. Some spinners have feathers dressing up the hook. Bass spinners often have rubber skirts surrounding the hook.

Several factors determine how well a spinner will work; color, size, and type of blade. The shape of the blade determines the speed and distance it will revolve around the shaft of the lure.

The blade flashes as it spins around the lure while being retrieved through the water. This flash looks like the reflection of sunlight off of a swimming baitfish. This flash can attract fish from far away.

Spinners also create vibrations which fish can sense. These vibrations both attract a fish's attention and can trigger a feeding response if the vibrations are erratic. The fish thinks that the spinner is a wounded baitfish trying to get away, so he rushes it.

I divide spinners into two categories: bass spinners, and trout spinners. Bass spinners are usually bigger with a 'v' shape and a dangling spinner, whereas trout spinners are usually straight. Trout spinners will catch bass and lots of other fish, but I've never caught a trout on a bass spinner. I bet you could use a bass spinner to catch a saltwater fish, but I've never tried.

*Assorted trout spinners*

Spinners are easy to use. You simply cast them out and reel them in. When a fish bites, it usually hooks itself. By varying the speed of the retrieve you can determine how deep the lure will run. Slow reeling will allow the spinner to stay deep, fast retrieve can bring the lure right to the surface. With practice you will learn to feel the pulsing of the spinner as it is retrieved. This is useful because it lets you know that the blade is spinning. If you do not feel the pulse of the lure the blade is not revolving. Fix this by raising the rod tip quickly.

You can also jig the spinner as you would a rubber worm or jig. I've caught a lot of bass by skimming the surface of a pond with a spinner. My little brother caught a big bass by practically dragging the bottom of a lake. You can fish the spinner any way you want and you'll probably catch some fish.

## *Topwater Lures*

Cling ching, cling ching, the ice cream truck is coming. You can't see it yet but you can hear its music and you start thinking about Rocky Road on a sugar cone. This is the way topwater lures draw fish to them. The splashing noises made retrieving one call the fish from all over the lake. They might not be close enough to see the lure right away but they move in with hungry anticipation.

Top-water lures work especially well along shorelines or near fish hiding places (something that provides cover) like docks, cattails, logs, etc. Cast the lure and allow it to float there for a moment. Often the splash of the cast will draw fish so give them a minute to start investigating what fell into the water. When you retrieve there are many things to try. Try giving the lure just a little twitch, nothing much, just enough to indicate to the fish that there is something struggling on the surface. Maybe give the lure a good yank, cause it to make some noise, then let it rest or just reel it in as fast as you can and force the fish to chase it (they will). Experiment, try imitating a frog swim (kicks and glides) and then a mouse, slow and even with occasional rests or a wounded baitfish that is attempting to swim only to lose strength and float twitching to the surface.

The best part of topwater fishing is the strike. Fish slam into topwater lures! Sometimes largemouth bass have hit my lure so hard that it has scared me to the point of almost dropping my rod.

Topwater lures generally are attention getters. They're designed to splash and make noise on the surface of the water, causing the fish to take notice and attack. Famous topwater lures include the Jitterbug, the Hula Popper, rubber frogs and mice, floating Rapalas, Zara Spooks, and many more.

*Topwater lures*

Top water lures are more effective in the morning or evening. They are also better in the spring and fall. If it is overcast or foggy they are worth a try. This is probably due to the limited light in these conditions causing the fish to hunt by sound.

*There is nothing like when a bass hits a topwater lure.*

I remember hearing a story, when I was little, about a Scandinavian fisherman. This fisherman earned his living by fishing the deep waters of the Finland countryside. The fishing had gotten slow and the old man began crafting a new fishing lure in hopes of coming up with something to improve his luck. He carved balsa wood into the shape of a little fish and painted it and attached hooks. He would pull it through the water and observe how in some ways it looked like a living, swimming fish and in some ways it didn't. He went back to carving it to get it just right. After many prototypes he finally had something that satisfied him as a replica of a little fish. So one morning he got in his boat with his lure and headed out to give it a try. It is said that he caught one hundred fish on that lure before it had been beaten up too much to use. But he went home and made more of them. His name was Lauri Rapala and now you can buy and fish a version of that balsa wood lure.

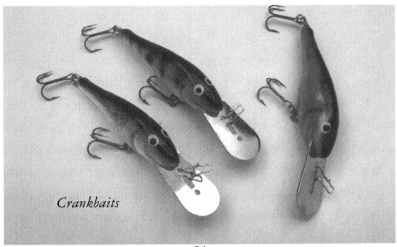

*Crankbaits*

Rapalas and other crank baits resemble fish and dive in the water as they are retrieved. Crank baits allow you to pick what depth you want to fish. They come in all sorts of colors and styles. The package will say what the crank bait is designed to do. Some float but when you reel them in their shape makes them dive. Others sink until you reel them in. Some are suspending and will hover unless retrieved.

To fish a specific depth with a sinking crankbait, count the seconds you let it sink before reeling it in. If you get a bite you will be able to try that depth again by letting the lure sink the same amount of time before reeling in. (Let it sink one second before retrieving it the first cast, then two seconds the next, three the next, and so on until you locate the fish).

Fish usually hit crankbaits hard. Because of the multiple treble hooks (three hooks stuck together), they nearly always hook themselves.

Try deep diving crankbaits in the hot summer months. These lures will swim near the bottom where the fish are likely to be.

## Spoons

It is said that a couple of friends were fishing from a boat while they were eating their lunch. One of the fishermen dropped his metal spoon into the clear waters of the lake. Because of the spoons shape it sank relatively slowly fluttering on the way down to the bottom. As it sank the fishermen casually watched it flash every time the sunlight caught a side of it. When it was nearly too deep to see anymore, it amazed the fishermen to see the shadow of a giant fish lunge for and devour the spoon.

The story says that the two fishermen started making lures that were in the shape of a spoon and that is where we get the spoon of today.

I don't think that this story is true but it might be. It seems to me that the spoons simplicity and effectiveness would have made it one of the first lures used by the very first fishermen.

The spoon's simple design (its shape resembles the bowl of a soupspoon) attracts nearly all species of fish. When retrieved with a series of stops and starts a spoon will flash and wiggle driving fish crazy.

Because spoons are usually heavier for their size than most lures, they can be cast much farther. This makes them the lure of choice on windy days when casting is difficult.

*Spoons will catch almost any kind of fish*

Have you ever walked around the shore of a pond or river and simply looked at what was there? I know it is hard to think about anything when there is fishing close by, but if you take the time to observe the shoreline you can learn a lot about fish. I'm always amazed at how many bugs are around. Whether it is an anthill or a bee on a flower or the mosquito in my ear there always seem to be insects. It makes sense that fish eat a lot of insects. Artificial flies imitate these various bugs.

In the morning, at dusk, or when the fish are jumping, it's a good time to try an artificial fly.

Although they are most commonly fished with fly gear, flies can be fished with the standard spin fishing set up. This is done with the aid of a clear bobber. The bobber can be filled partially with water giving you the weight required for casting. Attach the fly or popper several feet from the bobber. The bobber can scare fish so the longer the distance the better.

The fly is retrieved in a slow manner with frequent stops. Watch the area directly behind the bobber for swirls or movement. Since the fly is trailing the bobber, this is where the fish will be hitting it. As in traditional fly-fishing, the fish will reject the fly as soon as they taste it. So be ready to set the hook by raising the tip of the rod.

The difference between a fly and popper is that the popper is usually used to take bass and sunfish and is often much bigger and made partially out of wood. Poppers often imitate frogs or mice as opposed to insects.

# Chapter Eight:
## Sunfish

Every city in the country has a park with a pond in it; most of them contain sunfish. Although there are various kinds of sunfish, (bluegill, redear, crappie, etc.) let's just call all of them sunfish.

It's not difficult to catch sunfish. In lakes where they can be found, they are usually abundant and will bite nearly any bait presented in a natural manner.

Sunfish can be found near submerged trees, rocks, weeds, anything that gives them protection from predators. Sunfish will bite bait or lures. Common baits in-

*Sunfish will eat just about anything*

clude: salmon eggs, worms, grasshoppers, corn, hot dogs, cheese, marshmallows, basically anything that's the right size and will stay on a hook. They will attack small lures as well. Jigs, flies, poppers, rubber grubs, will usually get good response.

A fun way to get introduced to sunfish is with a bobber and bait set up. Tie a hook on your line, use a clinch knot. Once you've got your size ten hook tied on, put a single split-shot weight about eight inches above the hook. Attach a bobber about ten inches above that.

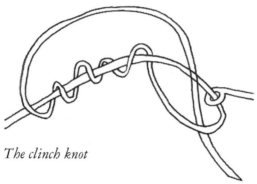

*The clinch knot*

You can use anything for bait. Sunfish aren't real picky, but some things work better than others. A salmon egg (Pautzkies) is good, or buy a can of corn at the store. This works and is much cheaper than salmon eggs. Grasshoppers, crickets, worms, or almost any bug that you want to catch and put on a hook will work.

Try to imagine what the fish eat naturally. If there are a lot of grasshoppers next to the pond, odds are that the fish are used to eating grasshoppers, and are just waiting for one to fall into the water. Use this information. Figure out where a grasshopper would fall in. What would it do? The closer you can imitate what a insect would do naturally, the more fish you will catch.

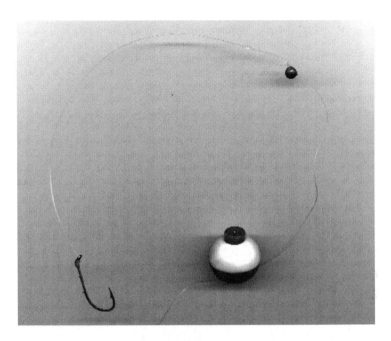

*Bobber rigging*

When you throw your line out, your bait will hang in the water below the bobber. The distance between your hook and bobber determines the depth. Remember to change the depth if you aren't catching fish. It might be that the fish are deeper or shallower than you've been fishing.

Make sure that your line does not have any excess slack in it. If you can make the bobber move by moving the tip of your pole, you don't have too much slack. This is very important because when a fish bites, you have to be ready to set the hook. Raising your rod tip quickly sets the hook. If there is slack line, when you pull up on the rod to set the hook, you'll just be pulling on loose line. The fish will spit out your bait and laugh at you. Waves may make your bobber drift towards you, creating slack line. Occasionally reel in slack to keep the line tight.

Watch your bobber for strange movement. You have to stare at it. If you look away, you will miss many strikes. When a bobber moves it means there is a fish messing with your bait. Sometimes, it just twitches. Sometimes it gets sucked completely underwater. Sometimes, the fish eat the bait, and start swimming. You'll see the bobber moving away.

When the bobber moves you never know how big a fish is under there. I remember fishing this way and my bobber began to twitch. I assumed it was a little sunfish but when I set the hook, it was a four-foot long alligator-gar.

When the fish bites, set the hook. Some fishermen wait a few seconds. Experiment and see what works best for you. Set the hook when you think that the fish has the bait in his mouth.

Getting the fish to bite and hooking them is only half the battle. You still need to get him to shore. When landing a fish, it's important not to simply crank it in, for a couple of reasons.

One, it might hurt the fish. There is no reason to rip the fish's mouth off, you will usually rip the hook out and lose the fish. And two, it is a bad habit to get into. You will undoubtedly fish for bigger fish than sunfish in your life. If you try to reel them straight in, they will break your line.

You will learn to feel the fish on the end of your line, to understand that he is trying to get away, trying to trick you. He will swim slowly to make you let down your guard, and then lunge through the water breaking your line or tearing the hook through his own lip to get away.

You will learn to give and take line with the fish, until one of you is too tired to continue and submits.

When fighting a fish, always keep the tip of your rod pointing towards the sky. This forces the fish to exert energy to bend the rod. If the rod is aimed at the fish, the fish is pulling against the strength of the line, which is not good: he will break it.

When fishing for sunfish, or any fish, it is good to learn all of these things, and practice is the way to learn them. Whenever possible, do everything yourself. For example, some people don't like to put a worm on the hook, so they ask their dad to do it. Well, they will never learn how. They will always need someone who will do it for them.

Taking the hook out of the fish's mouth is the same. Learn to do this yourself. It's not hard, it just takes practice. The secret is to figure out how the hook went in and then gently take it out in reverse. If a fish has swallowed the hook then use your needle-nosed pliers to gently remove the hook. If you can't get to the hook but the fish seems ok, you can cut your line. Cut it as close to the hook as you can. The hook will eventually rust away to nothing and the fish will be fine.

If you can tell that the fish has been hooked in such a way that you cannot take the hook out without fatally injuring the fish, then the fish must be killed to prevent its suffering. Do this by breaking the fishes backbone. Hold the fish in an upright position, and then strike the fish on the back of the head with a rock or club. Do this hard so you will surely kill the fish with one hit. This too, unfortunately takes practice.

There are many ways to catch sunfish. Using a bobber and bait is only one of them. You can catch them with flies or spinners or rubber worms or many other ways.

I will tell you a secret...a sunfish's favorite food is tomato worms. It's true, and I'm probably the only one who knows it. I experimented with them, and the sunfish worked themselves into a frenzy trying to eat the pieces of tomato worm on my hook.

If your parents have a garden with tomatoes in it, look on the leaves for green caterpillars with a circle marking on them and a stinger thing on one end. That is a tomato worm. They look kind of scary, but they have never hurt me. You'll need a scissors to cut them into pieces to put on your hook. If this is gross to you, try using a piece of hot dog for bait or a kernel of corn. Sunfish will eat almost anything.

Since sunfish are small, you will not probably want to keep them. They have to be scaled before they can be cooked and there isn't much meat on them. So throw them back. It's hard to let a fish go once you have caught it but you will feel proud when you see him swim away. But remember this: if you don't take care when releasing a fish, it can die.

First of all, always wet your hands before you touch a fish. Fish have a slime on them that protects them from disease. Handling a fish with dry hands rubs the slime off causing them to get sick and die.

The quicker you get the fish back into the water the better. Some fishermen don't even take the fish out of the water when they remove the hook.

Sometimes, after you've had a tough battle with a fish, it will be too tired to swim away. Hold the fish upright in the water and gently move him back and forth, forcing water through its gills. This will usually revive the fish and it will swim away.

It can be hard to decide to let a fish go. When I was little I wanted to keep every fish I caught to show everybody when I got home. I killed a lot of fish.

The fun of catching a fish is in the skill it took to accomplish, not in the meat or dead body of the fish. Let the fish go. You can go and tell everyone about him. Even if they don't believe you, you know that you caught him and you'll be proud of yourself that you let him go to live the rest of his life.

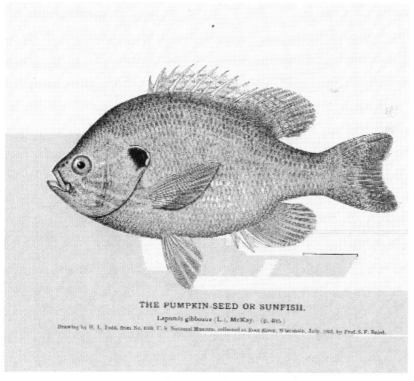

THE PUMPKIN-SEED OR SUNFISH.

Lepomis gibbosus (L.), McKay. (p. 485.)

Drawing by B. I. Todd, from No. 4188, U. S. National Museum, collected at Fox River, Wisconsin, July, 1881, by Prof. S. F. Baird.

# Chapter Nine:
# Bass

If the idea of a fish lunging through the water to nail your topwater bait appeals to you, try fishing for the largemouth bass.

My dad caught the first largemouth bass I ever saw by floating a grasshopper next to some cattails. Although not large, it jumped as he fought it and made the sunfish I was catching look small.

Largemouth bass hit lures hard. Sometimes the strike can be so sudden and violent it's almost scary.

Bass live in warm water where they share ponds and lakes with catfish, sunfish, carp, etc. Largemouths hide near tree stumps, weeds, lily pads, or anything that can give them cover to attack unsuspecting food.

Bass eat different things, but they really like crawdads, other fish, frogs, and insects. Since these foods

are normally found near shore, that's where you will typically find bass.

Bass respond well to lures. Often the faster it's moving the harder a bass will strike. There are tons of bass lures. The most popular include rubber worms, spinner baits, crank baits, and top water plugs.

Rubber worms take their fair share of largemouth bass. They come in all sorts of colors. Some of them have sparkles in them, some are scented, all of them catch bass.

The rigging used varies from place to place. The basic idea is to thread the rubber worm onto the hook and then to embed the point and barb of the hook back into the worm. This allows the worm to be fished "weedless." Since the hook isn't exposed, it doesn't catch on weeds. A sliding sinker is used above the worm. Rigged this way the worm can sink slower than the weight, allowing it to flutter as it falls.

Rubber worms are generally fished on the bottom. A fisherman raises his rod tip to lift the worm off the bottom and then allows it to fall again while reeling in slack line. This is known as jigging. It also works with jigs.

Rubber worms produce well during the summer months, when the fish are near the bottom where the water is cooler.

You can also use rubber worms with a bobber. Try this when the water isn't hot enough for the bass to be on the bottom. The retrieve is the same. It also works well to substitute a short rubber grub for the rubber worm when using a bobber.

There are many theories about which color worms work best. One study concluded that electric blue was the most effective. It seems to depend on the weather and the amount of light entering the water. Experiment with different colors until you have a personal favorite.

Of all the bass lures, the easiest to fish is the spinner. When the spinner is retrieved, the blade spins creating flashes. You do not need to give the spinner any additional action. The speed of the retrieve determines the spinner's depth in the water. If you think the fish are near the bottom, use a slow retrieve. The slower you reel a spinner, the deeper it runs. Use a fast retrieve when the bass are near the surface.

If one type of spinner isn't getting bites try a different color or size. Sometimes a yellow lure will cause the fish to jump out of their skins to bite when a black spinner hardly gets a second look.

After you've fished with spinners for a while, you'll begin to notice the steady vibration the spinner makes as it moves through the water. You can feel it pulsing through the rod. Sometimes you'll notice that the spinner is not creating the vibration. This means that the spinner is not spinning. In order to correct this simply jerk the rod tip up. This usually will get the spinner spinning again.

Many people attach pork rind strips to their bass spinners. Pork rind is a processed strip of pork that adds action. The strips can be bought at most tackle stores although not all carry them. You simply stick it on the hook and let it dangle in the current. You can cut them into different shapes to affect the way they wiggle in the water.

Much of a bass's diet consists of things that are found on the surface of the water; frogs, mice, injured fish, grasshoppers, and even snakes. Topwater lures imitate these creatures.

Commotion attracts bass to critters on the surface. Whether you are fishing with a rubber frog or a bass popper or a floating Rapala, the trick is to get the bass's attention. This is done by giving the floating lure some action.

*A couple of nice striped bass*

When fishing rubber frogs, duplicate the behavior of a frog that has jumped too far into the water and is trying to get back to the safety of the shore. It's a good idea to let the lure sit still for a moment after you cast. This allows the bass time to come over and investigate the splash he heard. Once the ripples have settled down, twitch the lure a little. Then reel it in a few feet and then let it rest again. Tease the bass into striking.

Keep your attention on the lure. Although you have no indication that a bass is eyeballing it, the water may erupt suddenly as the fish goes for the lure. This is exhilarating to say the least. Bass hit hard. When one takes your lure, you'll know it.

Rapalas, bass poppers, and imitation mice are all fished in a similar way. Jiggle 'em, wiggle 'em, make 'em jump and splash, anything to get the bass's attention. Of course you need to modify your presentation to represent whatever bait critter you are trying to imitate.

The mice imitations need to slowly swim toward shore. You might try letting them stop and rest a moment on their long swim.

Bass poppers only need to be twitched from time to time. They sometimes resemble a beetle that has landed on the water and can't swim or fly away.

Sometimes the bass aren't on the top of the water nor are they at the very bottom. For these times you might want to try a crankbait.

Crankbaits imitate baitfish and sometimes crawdads. The fish imitations need to struggle to swim down

towards the bottom only to give up and float back to the surface. This is what a natural injured baitfish would do.

Crankbaits have a plastic lip in front. This determines how deep the lure will run. If the lip is long the lure will usually run deep. If the lip is short, the lure will only dive a couple of feet as it is retrieved.

To fish a crankbait, choose one that will

*Nice bass*

76

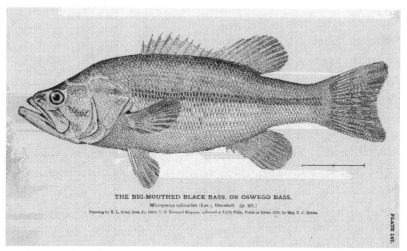

THE BIG-MOUTHED BLACK BASS, OR OSWEGO BASS.

*Micropterus salmoides* (Lac.), Henshall. (p. 101.)

Drawing by H. L. Todd, from No. 14544. U. S. National Museum. —Secured at Little Falls, Potomac River, 1874, by Maj. T. J. Hobbs.

swim at the depth you want. You may vary the speed of your retrieve. The faster the lure is reeled the quicker it will get to the depth it runs at. A stutter retrieve in which you reel and stop causes the lure to dart and then slowly float to the surface or sink to the bottom (depending on if it is a floating or sinking crankbait).

It can be helpful to file down the barbs on crank-baits. Barbs are the part of a hook near the point that curves out like a claw. Crankbaits usually come with either two or three sets of treble hooks making it tricky to remove the hook from the fish's mouth. Not only is it hard on the fish it can be dangerous to you.

I caught a big largemouth bass on a brown Rapala. While trying to take the treble hooks out of his mouth, he thrashed out of my grip. The loose treble hooks went all the way through my knuckle. I had to use a pliers in order to push the hook through my finger until enough of the barb was showing for me to cut it off and slide the hook back out the way it went in. It was no fun, plus I had to stop fishing for the day.

77

If the bass aren't biting, make them mad. Bass have tempers. They can be incited to bite when they aren't even hungry. In order to take advantage of this character trait; pick a spot on the lake and cast to it. Reel your lure in as fast as you can. Then do this again, same spot. Do it about 10 times. That bass will be so tired of that lure whizzing past his nose he will bite it out of anger.

While you are mastering the art of thinking like a fish, try to think like your lure. For example, if you were fishing with a floating imitation frog how do you think that frog would swim? If he was just killing time, he'd be doing frog kicks and glides. But what about if he is trying to get to shore because there is a huge bass after him? He'd probably swim quiet and slow when in deep water trying to not draw attention to himself but as he got close to the safety of shore he'd probably speed up to get away. You can manipulate your lure to act like a scared frog. This will look more natural to the bass and he'll attack it.

Lots of times I have reeled in lures so fast that they skim the surface of the water only to have bass try and swallow them. Sometimes my lure was moving too fast, and the bass would miss it. Do I slow down my retrieve so that the bass can catch it? No, that wouldn't be natural. Why would whatever the bass is chasing slow down so he could eat it? Always increase the speed of your lure as it nears shore. Bass will often hit right as you are about to pull your lure out of the water. Experiment, think like the fish and think like your lure, and you will undoubtedly catch some bass.

*I wonder why they call them "largemouth" bass?*

# Chapter Ten:
# Catfish

Of all the wonderful strange things in the world, catfish are one of the strangest and most wonderful. They lurk on the bottom of muddy water lakes and rivers. Their fleshy whiskers help them track down the scent of rotting meat. There are many different kinds of catfish. Some weigh over a hundred pounds, some are less than a pound, and some can walk on land.

A catfish is a scavenger, which means they like to eat dead things they find on the bottom, although they will also eat live food.

If you want to catch catfish, you're going to fish on the bottom with bait. Catfish hunt by smell, so your bait has to be smelly. Dead fish guts work well and sometimes worms or salmon eggs do the trick but if you really want to catch them, use liver. What could smell worse? But to a catfish it smells like cotton candy. I prefer using chicken livers because they usually come in a handy little tub and they are smaller than beef liver. Always be careful to keep the container of liver out of the sun while you are fishing or it will become too squishy to use.

Use a bottom rigging with liver for bait. Throw out your line and wait. Keep your line tight so you can feel the strike. If you're in a good fishing spot, with a lot of catfish, you rarely have to wait too long before they bite. Catfish have strong mouths so set the hook hard. Once hooked, a catfish will dive and pull hard. They don't jump but they fight. Even a small catfish can feel like a lunker.

*A catfish in his lair*

Once you get a catfish to shore be careful how you hold them when you remove the hook. They have sharp fins or spikes that stick up when you touch them. Grab hold of the fish so that the spines are sticking through the cracks in your fingers, and use a pliers to remove the hook. Really big catfish could close their mouths on your hands and maybe do some damage.

Besides liver, there are many good baits for catfish. Catfish will eat (among other things) dead fish, worms, cheese, shrimp, crawdads, mussels, grasshoppers, and homemade dough bait.

Dough bait is a favorite of many fishermen because they can create their own special concoction. I'm not going to reveal my secret recipe but I'll share a few ideas to get you started.

First make some dough. Mix flour with water to form a doughy consistency. Stir in whatever gross smelly things you can think of, to flavor the dough. I use ingredients like liver juice, cheese, molasses, sugar, salt, rotten meat, squid juice, and a couple of secret ingredients. You could leave this big yucky ball of dough in the sun to let it spoil a little, or maybe that's going too far. Chill this mess to make it stick together better. The catfish in your favorite fishing spot will let you know when you've got it right.

To fish with this stuff, pinch a little piece of dough and mold it around your hook. If you made it the right consistency it should stay on.

There's a superstition that catfish will bite your bait more often if you spit on it. This happens to be true. In an experiment, scientists tested catfish's reaction to different smells and the third favorite behind liver and worms was human saliva. So if you are superstitious, it can't hurt to spit on your bait, and it will probably help.

Although catfish live mostly on or near the bottom, you can fish for them at any depth. This is especially true in smaller ponds where a bobber rigging often works as well as a bottom rigging. However you fish for them, make sure to leave your bait in one place long enough for the catfish to smell his way to the bait.

Catfish can be just as exciting as other gamefish. Sometimes they can surprise you. When I was ten years old I was fishing a farmer's pond in Oklahoma. Using liver for bait, I had one hook and one weight on the line. While watching the water moccasins and snapping turtles in the lake, I had a bite. I didn't yank because it surprised me. I decided to leave my line out there and see if the catfish would bite again. About two minutes later I got another bite. This time I was ready. I set the hook and wow! The fish pulled real hard and I thought my line would break, but by taking my time I was able to get the fish to shore.

Only, when I got it to shore, it wasn't one catfish, but two! After examining them I figured out what happened. The first bite I felt was the first catfish. He bit the liver but he didn't spit it out of his mouth. It had gotten blown out of one of his gills so the line was going into his mouth, and coming out of his gill. The hook still held the liver and another fish came along and ate it. I hooked him, and reeled them both in; two fish on one hook!

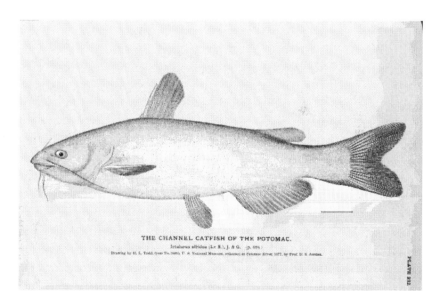

THE CHANNEL CATFISH OF THE POTOMAC.
Ictalurus albidus (Le S.), J. & G. (p. 698.)
Drawing by H. L. Todd, from No. 16675, U. S. National Museum, collected at Potomac River, 1877, by Prof. S. F. Baird.

Walleye love minows

# Chapter Eleven
# Walleye

Every fish has certain physical attributes and attitudes that can help you to catch them. Catfish hunt by smell so you use smelly bait for them. Trout spook easily so you must approach quietly. Bass are mean and bite out of anger. Walleye are no exception... they are sensitive to light.

A walleye's eyes are very good in dim light. This allows them to feed at night. However because their eyes are so sensitive, bright light hurts them. If it's sunny, the walleyes will go into deep water and you won't be able to catch them from shore. If it's windy, or cloudy, the walleye will come closer to shore to try and catch something to eat. If there's a lightning storm the walleye might not eat for days.

You can use this information about walleyes to catch them. Look for discolored water on sunny days to find walleyes. The dirty water doesn't let as much light through to the walleyes eyes. Or fish for them as the sun goes down and into the night. The spring and fall are better fishing than the summer because the sun isn't directly overhead.

Walleye spawn (lay eggs) in the spring and they don't usually eat for about ten days afterwards, but then the fishing can be real good. In the fall some of the biggest walleye are caught. They are eating in preparation for the winter and for spring spawning.

Walleyes are predators and like to eat live things like frogs, salamanders, minnows, worms, leeches, crawdads, and insects. I never fish with frogs or salamanders, but worms and leeches are good bait.

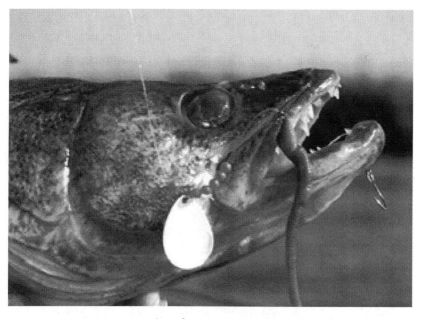

*A spinner tipped with a worm did the trick on this walleye*

85

Most people fish for walleyes near the bottom. The most popular bait is a jig with a worm, leech, or minnow added. Fish this with a jigging motion; a slow retrieve is usually best. Walleyes frequently bite softly, so it takes practice to detect a strike. Walleye often bite while the bait is sinking, so if your line stops moving or does anything unusual set the hook!

Crankbaits, jigs, spoons, streamers, and spinners all can be effective if fished slowly near the bottom. Often people will tip their lures with worms or minnows to make the lure more appealing. Take your time retrieving lures. If it feels like you hit a snag or weed then it's probably a Walleye.

Although Walleye are not great fighters, they can be fun to catch and are delicious. Because they are nocturnal (active at night), they offer 24 hour per day fishing. Who could ask for more than that?

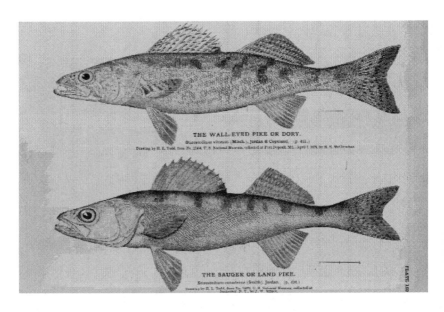

THE WALL-EYED PIKE OR DORY.

THE SAUGER OR LAND PIKE.

# Chapter Twelve:
## Trout

My fishing buddy Stan asked me to go fishing with him at a secret spot. It was a private lake, he said, but he knew someone who would let us fish there. Stan had been talking about this place for months before we finally made our way up to the mountains to give it a try. As we sat in Stan's car outside the gate that would give us access to the lake Stan was going stir crazy. Stan is 68 years young but he was acting like a kid. He had his face pressed up against the glass of the car and was sort of making a whimpering noise, similar to a hungry dog. I believe I said something like, "Gees Stan, the fish can wait a few more minutes before we go after them."

*Trout eat mostly near the bottom in rivers*

"Oh Paul" he said, "you don't understand at all what you are in for. This is not some average old fishing hole this is the real thing, it is paradise."

All spring Stan had been telling me stories about this private lake with the huge trout all over the place jumping clean out of the water. "They will eat just about any kind of fly you cast to them."

He really made it sound good but maybe he was exaggerating just a little. He claimed that the fish were as long as my arm and weighed five pounds and up. I didn't believe these stories because I have heard plenty of fish tales in my life. But the way he was going crazy in the car waiting for someone to come and open the gate for us made me curious as to just how big these trout really were.

Only five people would be allowed to fish the lake today and it was a big lake. I could see aerators pumping oxygen into the lake at various points so it at least looked like the fish were taken care of. Since there was next to no fishing pressure on the lake I figured it could hold some pretty big trout. When someone finally came to un-lock the gate we were more than ready to go. I surveyed the lake and noted that there were about 10 houses built near the water. These were summer homes and as far as I could tell they were all empty. Each house had a boat dock on the water.

When I asked where the best spots were, Mr. Fay the man who was graciously allowing us to fish at his lake said that the whole lake was a good spot. Anywhere from shore would be fine. I was getting more skeptical at this point because I couldn't imagine a lake where every

*Look at the spots on this trout*

spot was a good spot. Well, finally we walked down to the water, fly rods in hand. As everyone tied on their flies I made my first cast from shore. Nothing. I cast again, nothing.

The third cast was hit seconds after the fly landed on the water. A few minutes later I landed a 16-inch brook trout. That 16 incher was the smallest fish of the day. From shore I caught 6 fish over 25 inches, all rainbows. When one of these monsters felt the hook they thrashed so violently that it took all my arm strength just to hold on to the pole. It sounded like someone was slapping the water with an oar. It took about 10 minutes to land each of these fish. The entire time I fought each I thought that they were going to break my line.

It was amazing. To hook into fish that size was completely different from catching a normal sized trout. The lake was "catch and release" so we let all the fish go but man was it fun! My heart is racing just remembering that lake and all those huge trout.

Trout are wonderful in all sizes. A tiny little trout that jumps at your fly can make you as happy as a huge one. The trout is sort of the magician of fish. They appear out of nowhere and disappear just as quickly.

They're both delicate and strong. They can be fierce, yet they are mostly timid. They are beautiful. Their colors vary from river to river. Depending on the species, they can be shiny silver to deep brown to green to golden, and always freckled with spots. They thrive in cold clear water.

There are many different kinds of trout (Rainbow, Brook, Brown, Lake, Cutthroat, Golden, etc.) but let's just lump them together and say "Trout".

Trout can be found in cold water lakes, rivers, streams, beaver ponds, and even the ocean. Although most trout caught weigh less than two pounds, trout can get big.

THE RAINBOW TROUT,
Salmo irideus, Gibbons. (p. 473.)
Drawing by H. L. Todd, from No. 5060, U. S. National Museum, collected in the McCloud River, Cal. 1881, by Livingston Stone.

The easiest way to catch some species of trout is by fishing the bottom of a lake. I recommend that you try this before you attempt river fishing. It is a good place to start, and will familiarize you with the fish.

Although trout may be at any depth in a lake, you almost always find some near the bottom. Try using a bottom rigging.

This is the basic rigging people use to fish with bait near the bottom. Because the weight is secured below the bait, it is easier to feel strikes. The trout doesn't need to move the sinker for you to feel the bite.

Trout readily eat worms, crawdads, insects, salmon eggs, power bait, corn, shrimp, cheese, and even marshmallows. Cover your hook with the bait so that the trout doesn't feel the hook when he bites it.

If you don't get bites with one type of bait, try something else. Sometimes it's something as simple as the color of power bait you are using. If you aren't getting bites you might also try moving to a new spot.

When fishing on the bottom, there's no bobber to watch. As soon as you've let your bait sink to the bottom, slowly reel in a little line, just enough to take in the slack. With your line reasonably tight, you wait. Some people stand, I prefer to sit. I sit on a rock or whatever is there, so I can be very still while I try to detect a bite.

If you don't get any bites for a long time, reel in your line for another cast. As you retrieve your line, reel quickly so you aren't dragging your weight across the bottom because it will get stuck on a rock.

If you do get snagged (which happens to everybody) practice getting unsnagged yourself. One good way is to walk along the shore pulling your rod. This will often cause the snagged weight to pop free around the rock it was stuck on. Sometimes you'll have to break your line and tie on a new hook and weight. That's not so bad, it just takes time away from fishing.

If you don't get snagged reeling in your line, throw it out a different distance. If your first throw was a real far one, try one that isn't very far at all. Fish aren't always in the middle of the lake.

Trout bite in different ways. Often it's just a nibble you will probably not even feel, unless you are paying very close attention to your line. I usually put my thumb or forefinger on the line where it goes into the reel. This way if a trout bites, I can feel it with my thumb or finger.

Sometimes trout will nearly pull the rod out of your hands when they hit. Be ready to strike. As soon as you as you feel the bite, set the hook. If you were daydreaming and didn't do anything, wait a few minutes. Lots of times the fish will bite again and this time you'll be ready. If they bite once and then don't bite again, it might mean that they have taken your bait. Reel in to check and see.

When you hook a trout they fight hard. They also sometimes jump, which is very exciting. When a fish jumps, lower the tip of your rod. This puts a little slack in the line. Sometimes when fish jump they land on the line and get away. By giving them a little slack during jumps you avoid this.

Trout may be taken on many kinds of lures. The most common lure for trout is the fly. You can fish the fly with your spinning gear and a bobber or you may invest in a fly rod.

Trout are also frequently caught with spinners. My favorite trout spinner is the Panther Martin. Spinners, like spoons, are also good for trolling. So if you are in a boat you might try trolling a spinner.

### River Fishing for Trout

If you're fishing a river for trout, the first step is locating them. Trout like oxygenated water. When fast moving water splashes over a rock into the air, it absorbs oxygen. Trout like protection from predators. They also like the spots that are just out of the main current of the river. The trout will be behind rocks, under banks, or in pools and eddies. Trout face into the current watching for food to get swept down to them. Trout will dart into faster moving water to eat, and then quickly return to their hiding place.

It is possible to fish the bottom in rivers. Just find a deep pool or eddy and then put on enough weight to keep your bait from getting swept downstream. Rivers are much harder to fish than lakes. There are many snags along the bottom and with the current dragging your lure or bait along, you will get stuck often.

Some smaller streams and creeks have beaver ponds along them. These trout havens are created by dams that beavers build on streams to block the flow of water. Trout find safety from predators among all the logs and sticks surrounding beaver dams. There is also a good food supply as the stream brings insects down into the ponds.

Brook trout are often found in beaver dams. The trick to catching them is to be very quiet when approaching a beaver pond. The ponds are peaceful and still so any unusual vibration will spook the fish. Worms, spinners, and flies are probably the most effective baits for beaver ponds.

# Chapter Thirteen:
# Fly Fishing

Fly-fishing is by far the best way to catch trout in a stream. In my opinion, it's also the most enjoyable way to fish. Stream fishing is harder than other types of fishing. You must perfect many different elements to be successful. Your reflexes must be faster, your attention keener, your presentation better, your stealth stealthier. It is an art.

I remember when I caught my first fish on a fly. I was fishing the Cache a la Poudre River in northern Colorado. I'd been using spinners without much luck all day. As it got close to dusk the fish started jumping. I didn't have a fly rod so I tied a dry fly to the end of my line on my spinning outfit. I sort of swung the fly out as far as I could, which was about 3 feet. I got several strikes, which surprised me, since I hadn't had much luck with spinners. Finally I hooked a trout. It was beautiful and that started my love affair with the fly.

*Beautiful trout caught with a fly*

Most people don't learn to fish using a fly, but nearly all fishermen eventually try it. There is something magical about casting a fly as the sun sets over the mountains while fish are jumping all around you that is hard to find in other methods of fishing.

There are many things to learn in order to be a really fine fly fisherman but the basics are simple, and it only takes a little practice before you'll be able to catch fish. Once you understand the equipment and the differences between types of flies then you're ready to begin flyfishing.

Having a basic understanding of fly fishing equipment can help you to understand the various aspects of fishing with a fly. In a nutshell, there is the rod, the reel, the line, the leader, the tippet, the flyline backing, and the fly.

Most fly rods are made out of graphite. They used to be made of bamboo and some still are. Fly rods generally range in length from seven feet to ten feet. The most popular length is nine feet.

Fly rods are also distinguishable by weight. The weight and length of a fly rod are written on the side of the rod near where you hold on to it. Common fly rod weights are 3,4,5,6,7,8,9,10... The weight corresponds to how much the line weighs or the line "weight". This is not like monofilament lines pound strength. It's important to match the weight of the fly rod to the weight of the line. For example, if you had a 5-weight pole you would need 5-weight line. Matching the line weight to the rod weight allows for smoother casting. You decide which weight of rod to buy by what size fish you will be fishing for. Small fish like sunfish or small trout would require a 3-weight rod. Medium trout would be a 4 or 5 or 6 weight rod. Steelhead and salmon would be more like an 8,9 weight and then salt-water fish might be even more. The people that work in the fishing store where you buy your rod will be able to help you pick out the right weight rod for the size of fish you will be fishing for.

*Fly Reels*

The fly reel is also designed to match a fly rod's weight. Make sure that the reel you get is compatible with the weight of your fly rod.

The more expensive fly reels usually have advanced 'disc drag' systems. These allow you to adjust your drag to almost any tension you want. They also allow fish to run with line at a smooth, steady rate.

The less expensive reels usually have 'click drag' systems. These allow for less drag adjustment and they aren't as smooth as 'disc drag' reels. However, when you are first learning how to fly fish, having an expensive drag system is not important. Basically all the fly reel does is hold the line. The fishermen pulls line out when he is casting, and he usually fights the fish by pulling in line with his hand not by reeling the fish in unless it is a big fish. Of all the equipment involved in fly-fishing, the reel is probably what you should spend the least money on.

Fly line can be confusing because there are several different types. There are floating lines and sinking lines. There are weight forward lines and double tapered lines. There are different rates at which fly lines sink. There is also the weight of the line which, you recall, needs to be matched to the weight of your rod and reel. More expensive fly lines tend to float higher in the water, have a thinner diameter, and cast farther than less expensive lines. When you are first learning to fly fish, the cheap lines will work just fine. Most beginners start with a floating line. Floating line allows you to 'dry fly' fish or wet fly or nymph fish, so it gives you more options than sinking lines which are primarily used to fish deep fast moving water in rivers or to fish in a lake from a belly boat.

It's also a good idea to get a double tapered line as opposed to a weight forward line. A double taper line is tapered on both ends. This is useful because people often practice casting in a field or parking lot, which can damage the end of the line. If you have a double taper you can pull the line off of the reel and put it back on in reverse to use the undamaged tapered end. I recommend buying a floating, double tapered fly line to get started. Again, the people in the fishing store should be able to help you pick it out.

Fly line is only part of what connects the reel to the fly. There is also fly line backing, leader, and tippet. The order they go is as follows: the backing goes on the reel first then the fly line is tied to it. The leader is tied to the fly line and the tippet is tied to the leader. The fly is

*Nice salmon caught on a fly*

tied to the tippet. Fly line backing is a braided line that is thinner than fly line, which allows you to get much more of it on your reel than fly line. It is used as reserve line for the fish to pull out of the reel after he has already pulled out most of the fly line. This is so that if a fish runs, stripping line off of your reel, there is a lot of line for him to take. This gives you time to get him under control before he pulls all of your line out and you lose him.

The leader is a clear line that is tapered (starting out thick and getting smaller in diameter). Leader allows your fly to land on the water softly and is harder for the fish to see. Most leaders are either 7 1/2 feet long or 9 feet long. Shorter leader is easier to cast when you are first learning.

*Another big salmon*

The tippet is really the last couple of feet of your leader. It's thin and clear and also very flexible. It's hard for the fish to see and because it's flexible it allows the fly to move around in or on the water naturally. The reason I said that it is tied onto the leader is because as you change flies you are always cutting off a certain amount of tippet material. When you have cut off a couple of feet worth the fly won't look as natural in the water and it may even be hard to fit the line through the eye of the fly because it is too thick. At this point, it is necessary to tie some new tippet material to the leader.

Stores sell tippet material by itself in little spools of about 10 yards. Tippets are labeled 3x, 4x, 5x, 6x,etc. with 3x being stronger and 6x being less strong or thick. A rule of thumb to picking which size tippet to use is to divide the size fly you are using by 3. Whatever that number is should give you an idea which tippet is right for you. For example if you are using a size 12 fly (hook size), dividing by 3 gives you 4 so you would use a 4x tippet.

Once you have your rod, reel, backing, line, leader, and tippet set up; you are almost ready to fly fish. A couple of other tackle items will help get you started.

As with all types of fishing, fingernail clippers are wonderful because they allow you to cut your line precisely and with ease. Fly floatant is a substance you put on your dry flies. It helps to waterproof them so they won't get water logged and sink. You use this when you are dry fly fishing. People use fly sinkant when they are wet fly fishing to help make the fly sink. It just depends which way you are fly fishing which you use.

You will also need some tiny split shot weights. These are attached to the leader when you are nymph fishing. They help to get the fly to the bottom, which is the name of the game in nymph fishing.

Strike indicators are also used when nymph fishing. They are either little corks or pieces of foam, which you put on your leader. They float and they help you to tell if you've had a strike, since when nymph fishing your fly is on the bottom, sometimes it is hard to tell.

You're going to need something to carry all this equipment in, not to mention all your boxes of flies. A tackle box can be too cumbersome. Most fly fishermen use a fly vest to hold their gear. They have all sorts of pockets to put stuff in.

Once you have the basic equipment, you will need some flies. Flies come in all sorts of different colors, sizes, and styles. All flies share certain characteristics.

Flies are made on special hooks. The type of hook is determined by the kind of fly. For example, dry flies are tied on a lightweight hook. This helps to make them float. Wet flies, nymphs, and streamers are tied on heavier hooks that cause them to sink.

Choose a fly which looks like the insect the fish are feeding on. Most flies imitate a specific insect. An Elk Hair Caddis is supposed to look like the adult caddis fly. A Mosquito is supposed to look like an adult mosquito. I say 'adult' because insects go through different stages of life. During these stages the insect looks different. The bugs begin life in the water eventually emerging as a flying insect. It's similar to how a butterfly starts off as a caterpillar and then changes into a butterfly. Nymphs resemble the stage of life when the fly lives on the bottom of a river or lake. Wet flies resemble the stage as the fly makes its way to the surface of the water. Dry flies imitate the fly in it's adult stage when it flies above the water.

Dry flies have stiff hackle that sticks out from the shank of the hook. This stiff hackle makes the fly float on the surface of the water.

Wet flies have soft hackle that is set at an angle to the hook. These soft hackles flutter in the water making the fly look like it is alive.

Nymphs usually don't have any hackle and are sometimes weighted to help them sink quickly to the bottom. The body, wings, and tail of a fly all help to make the fly look like whichever insect it is supposed to imitate.

## Casting the Fly

Fly-casting is simple. It's the weight of the line that allows for casting. This may sound strange, but understanding this may make casting easier for you.

When spin-fishing it is the sinker and/or the weight of the lure that pulls the line out. Fly fishing usually uses no sinkers or heavy flies. The fly line weighs enough to pull more line out. This is why you have to swing the line back and forth over your head. You are letting a little more line out each time you swing your rod. Once you have enough line out, allow your line to settle onto the stream or lake, hopefully right above a hungry trout.

The only way to learn how to cast is to practice. It would probably help to watch someone, either someone fishing or someone on TV. There is a certain relaxed rhythm to fly casting that you can notice while watching someone. Start with only a little line out and begin by swinging your rod slowly. The biggest casting mistake is swinging the line back and forth too fast.

Sometimes people forget to allow the line to straighten all the way out before they reverse the direction of their swing. When they do this their line gets all tangled up. Always remember to stop your rod on the backswing and allow the line to straighten out behind you before you start swinging your rod forward. The more line you have out, the longer you have to wait for your line to straighten before reversing the direction of your swing.

It's not important to make long casts when fly-fishing. Often you will be fishing for a fish that is only a couple of feet in front of you. Of course, as with any kind of fishing, it's important to approach the water quietly so you don't scare any fish that are close to the shore.

Swinging your fly back and forth, not only lets out more line, and allows you to pinpoint where you will let your fly land; it also dries out your fly. This helps your

*Streamers imitate bait fish*

fly to float. If your fly starts to get water logged, swing it back and forth a couple of extra times to dry it out.

If you are out of rhythm, your fly will get snapped off while you are false casting (swinging your line back and forth). One way to avoid this is to swing your fly in a figure 8 motion during your false casts. This keeps a constant tension on the fly and eliminates the whip-snap action that can lose flies. When a fly gets snapped off there is a loud crack. This noise comes from the same reason a horsewhip makes a loud snap; the tip of the line breaks the sound barrier.

There are several different types of fly casts. They are all useful in different situations. When you need a very long cast you will use a double-haul cast. When there are too many trees around for a traditional cast, you might use a roll cast. These casts are more advanced. I recommend that you learn the basic fly cast and after mastering that, concentrate on different casting styles.

### Dry Fly Fishing

In all of fishing, I think my favorite feeling is the taste of anticipation one gets streamside as the sun goes down. The air gets cooler, people are locating their flashlights, making campfires, while I stand ready, and replacing the nymph I had been fishing with in the day with a dry fly. You could have had the worst day fishing with no bites, but you know that when the sun goes down the fish will come out to eat.

I like to watch the water for signs of fish. All day there has been no activity on the surface of the water and then as dusk settles in among the pine trees, the river comes alive. At first it might be a single jump, maybe not even a jump just a dimple in the rivers surface as a trout sucks down a tiny bug. But, as if the first jump was a signal that it is time to come out of hiding and eat, more trout start to jump. Pretty soon the whole river is alive with jumping trout. Now it is time to fish.

*Dry fly*

Dry flies float on top of the water. They look like a bug that has landed on the surface, or a dead one, which has fallen into the water.

When dry fly fishing a river, cast your fly upstream. Let it drift naturally downstream with the current. Keep your eye on your fly. Trout hit quickly. They also spit artificial flies out almost instantly, so you have to be ready to set the hook.

You'll find different aquatic insects at different times of year. Try matching the fly you are using to what flies are around at a particular time. If there are mosquitoes everywhere, try a Mosquito. If a big white moth tries to fly into your ear, you might try a large white fly.

Some flies aren't supposed to look like real bugs. They're called attractor patterns. Attractor patterns often work when lifelike patterns fail. The 'Royal Coachman" is an old standby attractor that continually produces. Flies with white wings, like a Royal Coachman, are easier to see when you are fishing at dusk.

Some people don't use small size flies because they don't think the fish will be able to see them. The fish can. Think about how small a mosquito or a gnat is, and remember that these are what fish normally eat. Most artificial flies are still big by comparison. On the other hand, don't be afraid to use larger flies either. Large flies are easier for you to see. Sometimes, fish will go after a big fly when the little ones aren't working and sometimes the bigger fish will eat a big fly but not a little one.

Although matching your fly to flies in the wild improves your chances, how you present the fly is even more important. With proper presentation, you could fish with a pink fly with green polka dots. The trick is to get the fly to float downstream at the exact speed of the river. That is the most important thing when fly-fishing. It sounds easy but it takes some practice. When your fly line floats slower or faster then your fly, it pulls it, creating "drag". Drag is the enemy of the fly fisherman.

You can eliminate drag by mending your line (flipping line up or down stream), casting to spots that allow for natural drifts, or raising your rod tip to lift line off of the water. A drag-free drift is the key to getting the fish to bite.

Cast your fly upstream from where a trout lurks. Watch your fly, if there is any drag on it, flip some line upstream to eliminate it.

Watch your fly and remember to set the hook as soon as a fish bites. The fish can tell immediately that the fly is a fake, so you need to hook him before he can spit it out. If you miss a couple of fish, don't worry about it, hooking a trout on a dry fly is tough. But it sure is fun.

### Nymphing

When I first started fly-fishing, I thought that fish ate most of their food at dusk, when I could see them jumping. This is not the case. Fish eat all day long, and most of the action goes on under the water. Of all the forms of fly fishing, nymphing is the most effective way to catch fish. Most of a fish's diet consists of bottom dwelling insects. A nymph imitates these aquatic critters.

Once you know how to fish with a nymph you will be able to take trout while everyone else is taking an afternoon nap.

Nymphing is very different from dry fly fishing. You cannot see your fly. The strike occurs underwater and is often very soft. Casting is more of a flip than long relaxed swings of the fly rod. Because of these differences it takes longer to master.

The equipment is basically the same as dry fly fishing with two exceptions. The fly or nymph is built to sink and is often weighted. Also, in order to perceive the strike, many nymph fishermen use strike indicators. Strike indicators are tiny, brightly-colored floats that are attached to the leader.

When you cast your nymph into the water, the leader and the nymph sink. The strike indicator will still be floating. The fisherman watches the indicator as he would a dry fly. If there is any strange movement, a twitch or a stall, the angler sets the hook.

When fishing a nymph it's very important that the nymph is near the bottom. Since there are currents in rivers, figure out how far the nymph will travel downstream before it has had time to sink to the bottom. If there is a nice deep pool that holds trout, cast well upstream of it so that the fly has time to sink before getting to the good spot.

Sometimes the river is too swift for the nymph to ever reach the bottom. In these situations add weights to your leader. Tiny split shot work the best. Add enough sinkers, about 10 inches above your nymph, to get your fly to the bottom. This will detract from the presentation

*Nymphs are fished as close to the bottom as possible*

of your nymph, but it's unavoidable. If your nymph is not near the bottom you won't get many bites.

With added weights casting becomes even trickier. I tend to swing the nymph out instead of casting. And it's hard to get the fly out very far.

There are several approaches to fishing the nymph once it has been cast. Dead drift nymphing means allowing the nymph to float along with the current. The nymph imitates a bug that has lost its grip on a rock and is being swept downstream. As in dry fly fishing, prevent the line from pulling the fly, creating drag.

When fishing a deep pool it can be desirable to give the nymph some action. Do this by stripping in line a couple of inches at a time. You can also move the nymph by twitching the end of the rod. After the nymph is in a good spot, the fish can be incited to strike by raising the rod in a slow, steady motion. This makes the nymph look like it's trying to swim towards the surface of the water. Fish strike because they think the nymph is trying to get away.

Detecting the strike is like catching a floating bit of dandelion fluff. You will get many bites as your nymph glides along the bottom. The fish seldom strike hard however. It's usually a gentle almost imperceptible movement of the leader that indicates a bite. Strike indicators help, but even if you are staring right at the indicator, you'll miss many strikes. The secret is to raise the rod any time you sense anything. If the indicator stalls, twitches, or does anything strange, set the hook. You will learn that this is almost always a fish.

Of the many different nymphs to choose from, my favorites are the "Bead Head Hare's Ear" and the "Bead Head Pheasant Tail." The bead helps to make the nymph sink and seems to make the nymph more attractive. I also like to tie my own nymphs and create new patterns.

The most important part of a nymph is the tiny hairs that stick out from the body. These resemble tiny gills on the insect and flutter in the water. This is what the fish are looking for. Every fly I tie has tiny little hairs or feathers sticking out of the body.

# Chapter Fourteen:
# Tying Flies

When it's winter, and there is no where to go fishing, it can be fun to tie flies for the spring. It takes practice to be really good at it but anybody can tie flies that will catch fish. It's especially fun to catch a fish on a fly you made up.

You will need a book that shows you how to tie flies. Get a book that shows you different patterns and how they are tied. Some of the books that you might get do not let you in on the little secrets that can make fly tying easier.

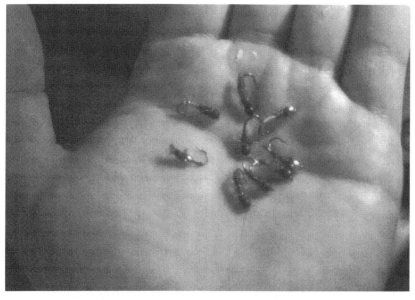

*These are some nymphs I made up*

When I started tying flies I used bigger than normal hooks. This was partially due to the fact that I didn't have a vise so I had to hold the hook in one hand while tying the feathers on with the other. But it also made it easier to learn how to make different patterns because I could see what I was doing. Try using larger hooks than the books recommend when you first get started. Once you learn the particular fly pattern then you can try it in smaller sizes.

Some people have problems tying tails on. The tail material tends to roll around the shank of the hook. One of the secrets to tying flies is to vary the tension of the thread wrap. The trick is to wrap the thread over the tail several times softly without pulling to hard and then gradually increase tension to secure the tail. This system of changing thread tension works for other parts of the fly as well.

The tail is used as a balancer and helps to hold the fly in the best position in relation to the hackle, practically keeping the hook out of the water. If you make the tail too long or too short it won't be a balanced fly.

You can use any material that you want to tie flies. Just because some book says to use moose-mane or peacock hurl or something, doesn't mean you have to. Use whatever you want. I have used dog hair, my own hair, cattails, carpet fibers. One of my favorites is Christmas tree tinsel. Experiment with whatever you find lying around. Some things will work better than others will.

Hackle quality is important. If your flies are not floating well your hackle may be too soft. Getting good hackle will improve how well your fly floats.

Many fishermen pinch the barb on the hook flat while they are tying the fly. Remember that having the barb bent down makes it much easier to remove from the fish's mouth. It also gives a released fish a better chance of survival. And if you ever get a fly stuck in your shirt or skin you will be glad that the barb is bent flat.

There really are no rules. Fly tying is for fun and if you can catch fish with it, it is a great fly.

# Chapter Fifteen:
# The Ocean

When I think of the ocean I think of old fashioned sailing ships filled with bloodthirsty pirates. I imagine the noise of the seagulls and the smell of the salt. I can almost feel seasick picturing the rise and fall of the boat.

There is something magical about the ocean. First off, it's so huge it looks like it goes on forever. It's so powerful that humans have never made a boat that it can't crush. It also smells great. But mostly it holds a lot of big fish.

*The ocean is full of big fish*

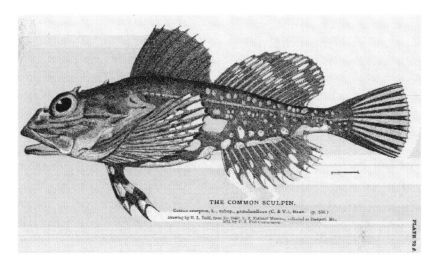

THE COMMON SCULPIN.

*Sculpins are fun to catch, even if they are a bit strange looking*

Saltwater fishing uses the same principles as freshwater fishing. You have to know what the fish eat and where they are. Then imitate their natural foods.

The equipment is different. Mostly it's heavier. Instead of using 6 lb. test line you would probably use 15 lb. and you would want a reel and rod designed for that weight. Remember that most rods and reels have the recommended line size written right on them.

There are different ways to fish the ocean. You can fish from shore, which is called surf fishing. You can fish from a dock or from a pier or jetty. You can go out in a boat and troll or bottom fish. You can even fly fish.

*Fishing the Docks*

If you have never fished in the ocean, the best place to start would be from a dock. A dock is where all the boats are tied up. Docks are made of wood and are usually floating on the water. This is cool because as you stand on the dock you can feel the ocean lift it up and down.

Fish live under and around the dock. The dock offers protection from predators, and fishing boats spill fish bits into the water when they unload their daily catch.

Use fish parts as bait. Then drop your line over the side of the dock into the water and wait. It usually takes a whole 10 seconds before you get a bite. That is one of the reasons it's so fun. The other is that you never know what you are going to catch. Most of the time you will catch sculpins, a small ugly fish. Sometimes you'll catch a crab. Until you know what you are doing, keep your fingers away from big crabs. They can pinch painfully hard.

Larger fish swim around docks as well, be ready, you could hook into something so big it could pull you in.

## Fishing the Surf

Fish the surf for perch, striped bass, sharks, etc. It's really fun, but like all ocean fishing, it can be dangerous.

Part of the fun is seeing how far out you can cast, and since you will be using a big long pole with a lot of weight you can cast awfully far. Some fishermen wade out into the surf to cast and some stand in the waves while waiting for a bite. There is nothing wrong with this but you have to be careful. Waves vary in intensity and speed and if you're not careful they can knock you over or even cover your head.

*Surf fishing is a chance to show off your casting ability*

There are also undertows, which are very scary. Undertows are currents underneath the waves. They pull out towards the open sea. Most beaches that have strong undertows are marked and often you are forbidden to wade on these beaches and definitely no swimming or surfing. If you get sucked down by an undertow it can pull you miles into the ocean before it lets you to the surface. By that time you're shark bait anyway so be careful and always have someone with you.

*Baits*

Common baits for fishing the surf are sandworms, mussels, clam neck, or sand shrimp. All of these creepy baits catch fish.

Clam necks are sold in tackle stores along the coast of the ocean, especially near bays and docks. They come in a little Styrofoam cup. They are easy to put on the hook and stay on well.

*Clam necks stay on the hook better than sand shrimp*

Sandworms are a little different. Many stores sell them, but it's fun to catch them yourself. They live in the wet sand. When you find one you'll know it. They are gross and weird and

118

have lots of legs like a giant centipede. Some of the sandworms I've pulled out of the wet sand were longer than my shovel. Cut or break them into bite-size pieces to put on your hook. Fish love them.

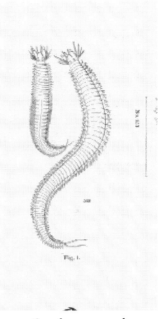

Mussels are similar to clam necks. They come in a little cup. They work well. If you walk along any rocky beach you could probably find some stuck on the rocks.

Sand shrimp are my favorite bait for surf fishing. They look like little aliens. Sea perch love them, but because

*Sand worms make great bait when fishing the surf*

they are soft they come off the hook easily. Hook the perch on the first bite or they will steal your bait. Sometimes I split the sand shrimp in half making it easier to put them on the hook.

All of these baits are wonderful as long as they are fresh. Just remember that fish-bait and the sun do not mix. Keep your bait in a cool bucket maybe even with ice because once they get hot they die, smell, get mushy, and then they won't stay on the hook at all.

It also seems like everybody wants the bait, so you need to keep it sealed so you don't get attacked by seagulls or crabs or seals or whatever.

There are some places along the beach that are better than others. Look for changes in the coloration of the water. Darker areas usually are deeper. If you can find a spot near shore where the water is much darker than the rest of the surf, you will have found a drop off. These areas tend to attract more fish than shallow spots.

When surf casting it's important to get your bait out pretty far. I usually run towards the water and cast when the waves are going out. Then I run back as the wave chase me, letting out line as I run.

Keep your line tight so you can detect bites. The fish generally bite hard, but with the movement of the waves it can be hard to tell.

As with any kind of fishing, the trick is to visualize what is going on under the water. Along the shore the fish are eating the shrimp, worms, and crabs that are uncovered with each crashing wave. There are also larger fish feeding on the fish that are eating what the waves uncover.

Fish in the ocean eat mostly other fish. Therefore whether you are fishing in the surf or from a boat or from a dock or jetty, baitfish and lures that look like baitfish are the most consistent producers.

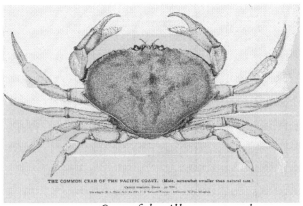

*Ocean fish will even eat crabs*

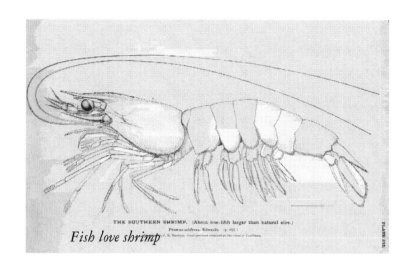

THE SOUTHERN SHRIMP. (About one-fifth larger than natural size.)
*Penæus setiferus, Edwards. (p. 821.)*

*Fish love shrimp*

## Fishing from Jetties

Jetties are another fun place to fish from. Jetties are long man-made rock piles that head out into the ocean a ways. Jetties are good fishing because they allow you to fish much deeper water than you otherwise could from shore. However, they are very dangerous! The ocean sends "sneaker waves" along the sides of jetties. Sneaker waves are sudden waves that are much larger than the other waves. There is no way to tell when one of these is coming, and they often will cover the entire jetty with water. These waves can easily knock you off of the rocks and into deep water. Even experienced adults will tie ropes around their bodies to protect from getting swept into the ocean. Every year people die from getting knocked off of jetties. It is much better to try your luck from the beach or a dock than to risk your life on a jetty.

# Chapter Sixteen: Lunkers

Everyone dreams of catching a world record fish. Whenever a bobber ducks under the water, visions of gargantuan trophy fish are conjured up. You would think that it's merely luck that allows you to hook into a prize fish. If this were the case than you wouldn't have people who consistently catch the big fish. But there are these people.

To catch a lunker, it helps to be lucky. But you can increase your chances of catching a huge fish by trying to catch them. Some people assume they are always trying to catch a big fish, but often they are just fishing for fish, any fish, and not just big fish.

Big fish are more experienced than small fish. The reason they are so big is that they haven't been caught. They aren't likely to be tempted by the same salmon egg or spinner they have already seen over and over.

People switch fishing spots away from big fish all the time. When a big fish moves into an area, the smaller fish try to get away. They hide or leave and they don't eat. If the fishing gets bad suddenly, don't change spots, a lunker might be right in front of you.

Big fish like big food. They don't waste energy chasing mayflies or salmon eggs. They want to catch something that's going to fill them up. When fishing for big trout, I use big streamers like the "muddler minnow." Trout stake claims on the good feeding spots in rivers.

The biggest trout gets the best spot. You can pretty much tell where the big ones are. It's just a matter of not spooking them, and offering a big fly with no drag.

Big bass eat big minnows, so you can fish with Rapala and other baitfish imitations that are 10 inches long, and you can fish them fast. Remember that you can get a bass mad enough to bite almost anything. I've seen big bass try to eat those black and red birds that live in the cattails. I saw a video that showed a bass try to eat a baby duck.

With any kind of fish, if you are trying to catch a lunker then you need to act like it. You need to use heavier line, a stiffer rod, and big bait or lures. Of course these are just guidelines. Luck has a lot to do with fishing. You never know, the next time your bobber ducks under water, it just might be a new world record.

Once I was fishing a river below a dam. Earlier in the day the dam had been turned off so that no water would come through it. They do this from time to time to clean the turbines in the dam. When they do, the river starts to dry up and all the fish are trapped in pools of water. It's fun to fish in these pools because they are full of fish. I was using a bobber and a worm, not even a nightcrawler, just a worm, when my bobber started to dance around like some little fish was nibbling on it.

Then all of a sudden the bobber went under the water real fast. I set the hook and immediately a huge gar jumped. He must have been about four feet long. I fought him for a little while until he started to get tired. I got him right to the shore but my dad couldn't quite reach him with the net and he grabbed a hold of my line to try and pull him closer. But by grabbing onto my line he eliminated the effectiveness of my drag system. The fish was just too big and he broke the line. I got to see him close up, and he was big! That time I was just lucky that the lunker went after my worm. The next time I fish in that area I will be using heavy equipment and concentrating on catching giant alligator gar.

# Chapter Seventeen:
# Other Fish

The world is full of cool fish. The species we've discussed can be found in most states but certain locations hold fish that boggle the mind in their size, shape, and ferociousness.

## *Carp*

In the same lakes that contain catfish, bass, and sunfish, you may find carp. These golden brown fish grow to weights of 70 lbs. The scales on these monsters can be the size of a quarter. They look like giant goldfish.

Carp are primarily vegetarians, feeding on grass, weeds, and berries. To catch one try a bobber/ hook rigging with corn, doughbait, half-boiled potato, canned peas, or a worm as bait. Be patient, carp use their sense of smell to find food so it can take a while.

THE CARP MULLET.

Although some people don't appreciate carp, they are wonderful game fish. They fight really hard. I like carp because you can find them easily. It is much harder to locate a 20-pound trout or bass than a giant carp. Sometimes, when they are spawning you can see them right next to shore.

*Carp will eat worms, but they love half-boiled potatoes*

## Muskie

Known as the "wolf" of freshwater fishing the Muskie is an awesome fish. They grow up to 5 feet in length. Their teeth can cut through standard monofilament line so a wire leader is necessary. A ferocious predator, Muskie lie in ambush for big meals (ducks, snakes, trout, etc.). Large crankbaits and topwater lures retrieved quickly cause these beasts to attack. They often bite through lures.

## Salmon

Salmon are born in freshwater rivers. They swim down the river to the ocean where they grow up to 100 lbs. (depending upon the species). They then return to the exact same river where they were born to mate and lay their eggs. While in the ocean, salmon can swim up to thousands of miles away before returning.

You can fish for salmon while they are in the ocean or while they are in the rivers. In the ocean salmon are caught from boats with lures or bait. Spoons, plugs, and various squid imitations work well. Strips of herring or whole squid will also catch them. In rivers anglers use salmon egg clusters, spinners, spoons, and flies. Salmon are a popular food and are fun to catch. They jump when hooked. When salmon are in the rivers tease them into striking like you would a bass.

## Steelhead

Steelhead are similar to salmon in that they live part of their lives in freshwater rivers and part in the ocean. A steelhead is a rainbow trout that swims out to sea where it gets big and turns silver. Fish for steelhead like you would fish for salmon. Steelhead grow up to 50 lbs. but most are around 8 lbs.

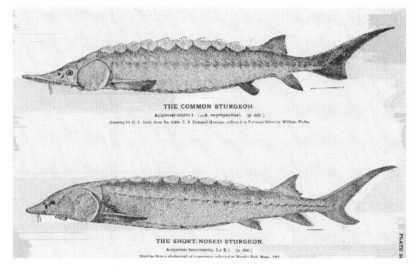

THE COMMON STURGEON.
Acipenser sturio L. (=A. oxyrhynchus). (p. 693.)
Drawing by H. L. Todd, from No. 21689. U. S. National Museum, collected on Potomac River by William Wilson.

THE SHORT-NOSED STURGEON.
Acipenser brevirostris. Le S. (p. 696.)
Drawing from a photograph of a specimen collected at Wood's Holl, Mass. 1871.

## Sturgeon

Half fish half dinosaur, sturgeon live in coastal rivers. These gargantuan fish produce roe (eggs) which is processed into caviar. Sturgeon grow up to 14 feet in length and weigh as much as a piano. They are bottom feeders like a catfish. They will bite on whole fish. They also eat river moss. Fishermen roll this seaweed into a ball around their hook to tempt these prehistoric monsters. Sturgeon fight tough and sometimes jump. They can live as long as a man.

129

## *Sharks*

Sharks stir the imagination, inspire fear and curiosity, and intrigue anglers everywhere. There are many different kinds of sharks and they are amazing. Shark's teeth are serrated like a steak knife. When they are dulled they fall out and a new one replaces it with a razor sharp edge. Sharks can smell blood in the water from miles away. They also have an electromagnetic sense that helps them to locate prey. In place of scales they have leathery skin. Their eyes have a protective lid, which covers them when they attack food. They can regulate their body temperature allowing them to hunt in different water depths
. Sharks feed on everything from crabs to fish to seals and sea lions. Some are dangerous to man and some aren't. They are all cool.

You can catch sharks from the surf or from a dock or jetty. They are also caught from boats. They are delicious. Some are small; some, like the great white, can weigh over 2,000 lbs. They are the perfect hunting machine.

Sharks are the only animal that doesn't get cancer. The largest fish is the whale shark, which can reach lengths of 70 feet. Whale sharks eat plankton.

*Shark!*

131

## Peacock Bass

The Amazon River flows through the jungles of South America. Besides the snakes, jaguars, and natives that hunt monkeys with blowguns, there are exotic fish. The peacock bass hunts in these waters. This fish hits a lure so hard it can pull the rod out of your hands. Although few Americans ever get the chance to fish for them because of their remote location it is well worth the trip. Just watch out for the giant tarantulas.

## Piranha

In the same waters lurks a fish which, although relatively small, hunts with ferociousness that inspires nightmares. The piranha looks like a sunfish with one noticeable difference... its numerous teeth. These fish can be caught with bait or lures but be careful removing the hook, again because of their teeth.

# Chapter Eighteen:
# General Information

There are several things I've learned the hard way that I will relate, in hopes of sparing you similar misfortune.

Don't ever step on wet rocks. Often when fishing rivers I will step out on rocks that are surrounded by water in order to get closer to the pool I want to fish. Sometimes the river water laps up on one edge of a rock. Never jump to a rock that is wet. The water makes them very slippery, not just a little slippery, but super slippery. If it starts to rain while you are fishing then all the rocks will be slick. A hard fall on the rocks or into the river can ruin even the best day of fishing.

It's important to be careful when you are by yourself and to always plan ahead so that people know where you are going and when you will be home. This is so that if you don't come home, they know to come look for you.

If you take the couple of easy steps to staying safe, then fishing can be a lot of fun. As a matter of fact, I think it is the most fun thing to do in the world. You get to be outside, surrounded by frogs and snakes, and worms and birds and everything that nature has to offer. Fishing never gets old. Every lake, river, and beaver pond holds the possibility of adventure. Every bite could be a record fish. Fishing gives you time to think, time to notice things, time to relax.

I hope that someday the smell of salmon eggs makes you happy.

# Epilogue

Stealing away like a secret, the old man made his way for the dock, his bones creaking with each step. The rain fell upon his cheeks with an infrequency of the most annoying nature. His body showed the signs of a long and eventful life. But as he approached the deep water you could see the little kid in him. The kid that never grew up and through fishing got to come out and play.

His blue eyes scanned the waves. Fish signs were easy to find if you knew what to look for. "Where little fish school, big fish feed," he mumbled to himself.

The wind kicked the smell of salt off the waves and rocked the little boat with firm hands. On the ocean, you are always a guest.

With care he set his line. He took pride in the perfection of his knots; the Bimini Twist, the Huffnagle, knots to maintain the continuity of what joined his will to the fishes. Taking his time, savoring the anticipation, he prepared to fish.

With the shore long since out of sight, he cut the motor. Years ago he decided to fish without the aid of the boat even though it wasn't as effective. With his cast made, he settled into his chair, letting the lure sink before retrieving it.

The cast offered nothing, no information except that there were no bites. Again and again he offered his lure with the same results. He felt the lure working through the water. Each crank of the reel handle offered the promise of a fish.

The strike hit like lightning.

Sinewy muscles came to life underneath the sun dead skin of his forearms. His boat lurched toward the fish. The rod bent, straining with the pull of the fish, or the old man, depending upon how you looked at it. The diving fish stripped line only to give it back as the fisherman fought on.

The depths would not allow a glimpse of the monster. In a sudden charge, the fish dove stripping line and not stopping. The old man watched the last of his line snap as the fish pulled it all out and as quick as that it was gone.

The fish never revealed his size or species. It took the lure, the carefully tied knots (which held), and all the line to the bottom of the sea.

Setting his gear down and starting the motor, the old man headed back to shore. Fishless, lineless, worn out from the battle, the old man smiled the whole way in.


THE END

Made in the USA
Middletown, DE
07 July 2017

$7.95

This book will make everyone a better fisherman, but it caters to the angler who still enjoys Saturday morning cartoons and raising earthworms in the backyard.

-Paul Amdahl

"The Barefoot Fisherman is an enthusiastically recommended 'how to' guide for preparing neophyte fishermen on getting the most out of their fishing trip!"
**Jim Cox**
**Midwest Book Review**

"I kept wishing that he had written the book 50 years ago so the kid in me could have learned from this master fisherman."
**Jim Fay**
**Co-Author of Parenting with Love and Logic**

"For those already familiar with the basics of fishing, this is the book to read."
**School Library Journal**

"The Barefoot Fisherman is the kind of book every kid should read."
**Gordon Charles**
**Woods and Waters Magazine**

MADE IN THE USA

Cover Design By:

FIGURE of SPEECH INC.
MARKETING COMMUNICATIONS FIRM
www.figure-speech.com

ISBN 9780692202142

London and Stout Publishing

9 780692 202142